This journal belongs to...

FUTURE

Future PLC Richmond House, 33 Richmond Hill,
Bournemouth, Dorset, BH2 6EZ

Editorial
Editor **Rebecca Greig**
Designer **Laurie Newman**
Editorial Director **Jon White**
Senior Art Editor **Andy Downes**

Contributors
Olly Tew, Natalie Denton, Julie Bassett, Jo Cole, Jill Robinson, Madelene King,
Steven Mumby, Steph Guttery

Cover images
Getty Images

Illustrations
Katy Stokes, Jordan Travers, Getty Images

Photography
All copyrights and trademarks are recognised and respected

Advertising
Media packs are available on request
Commercial Director **Clare Dove**
clare.dove@futurenet.com

International
Head of Print Licensing **Rachel Shaw**
licensing@futurenet.com

Circulation
Head of Newstrade **Tim Mathers**

Production
Head of Production **Mark Constance**
Production Project Manager **Clare Scott**
Advertising Production Manager **Joanne Crosby**
Digital Editions Controller **Jason Hudson**
Production Managers **Keely Miller, Nola Cokely,
Vivienne Calvert, Fran Twentyman**

Management
Chief Content Officer **Aaron Asadi**
Commercial Finance Director **Dan Jotcham**
Head of Art & Design **Greg Whitaker**

Printed by William Gibbons, 26 Planetary Road,
Willenhall, West Midlands, WV13 3XT

Distributed by Marketforce, 5 Churchill Place, Canary Wharf, London, E14 5HU
www.marketforce.co.uk Tel: 0203 787 9001

Go Plastic Free First Edition
© 2019 Future Publishing Limited

Connectors.
Creators.
Experience
Makers.

Future plc is a public
company quoted on the
London Stock Exchange
(symbol: FUTR)
www.futureplc.com

Chief executive **Zillah Byng-Thorne**
Non-executive chairman **Richard Huntingford**
Chief financial officer **Penny Ladkin-Brand**

Tel +44 (0)1225 442 244

Widely
Recycled

ipso.

For press freedom
with responsibility

Contents

A NOTE FROM THE EDITOR

'I'm not very good at recycling, so won't bother', or 'I don't really understand what I can recycle, so I won't waste my time' – these are both excuses I'd use to justify not recycling. Then I'd just laugh off my utter stupidity with a shrug. It's so easy to make excuses. It's even easier to make excuses about issues that you don't think directly impact you. You might not see marine life suffering from our selfish and constant use of plastic, but I can assure you that it's happening. The plastic problem is very real and it is not going to go away any time soon.

Like many people in our world, I used to cling on to the excuse that because the majority of people aren't changing their ways then why should I? Not everyone else is giving up single-use plastic, so what difference am I going to make? My daily disposable coffee cup isn't really going to have a direct effect on the environment, so why do I care? If everyone continues in this vein we are going to have an even bigger problem on our hands than we do now – and

it's already pretty bad. The time to act is now. Actually, it was probably time to act yesterday, or even a few years ago, but let's not put it off any longer. Let's be proactive together and make a difference today.

This will sound terrible, but I'm not really an animal person and, until recently, whenever someone tried to preach at me about the environment and global warming, I would feel my eyes rolling into the back of my head. I'd always known that this was a huge issue that needed to be taken seriously, but my immediate selfish thought would be, 'It still doesn't really affect my day-to-day life, so there's no point causing such a fuss'.

Maybe I felt this way because environmental protesters and activists have been given a bad reputation. A lot of us will immediately picture a grubby-looking hippy covered in flowers and peace signs floating along, demanding that we learn to love the world and everyone in it. However, that just isn't the case – anyone and everyone in their right mind should really be fighting

against the damage that is being inflicted on our planet every day. You'll probably never see me out on the streets with a placard protesting against environmental policies, but even I know that we have a plastic problem that isn't going to go away any time soon. Going plastic-free and caring for the environment isn't just for activists and campaigners – every single person is accountable. Every single person has the capacity to make a change, and every single person should, no matter how inconvenient it might feel.

Change doesn't happen at once. It has to be done in small increments – you and I can be a part of this change. You might feel powerless, but every small, seemingly insignificant contribution adds up and will help us to change the world for good. It will just take time.

Going plastic-free is so difficult, and I'll be honest, I'm not quite there yet. But I am doing my best to be better. If everyone did their best to use less plastic then we'd see a significant improvement very quickly. Much like going on a diet, taking the extreme approach of cutting everything out instantly is not going to be sustainable or easy for anyone. Instead, start with small and simple changes, such as buying a reusable coffee cup or an aluminium water

bottle. Don't feel bad if you slip up at first, just don't give up. It's all about forming a new habit – eventually avoiding plastic will become your norm. I initially thought that my biggest problem was coffee cups and water bottles for the gym, so I bought reusable alternatives for both. However, when I really looked around my kitchen and my flat I realised that there is so much that I didn't even notice. Now that I've taken notice, I can act – and so can you.

Some plastic is genuinely unavoidable – this might change soon – so don't feel bad if, for example, your medication comes in a plastic blister packet because there might not be an alternative. Instead, make sure that the plastic you can't avoid is disposed of responsibly. Similarly, supermarkets are beginning to take notice of their consumers' growing concerns about plastic, and there are zero-waste shops popping up all the time. Almond & Co, who you'll read about later, is a Bournemouth-based shop just around the corner from my flat and has been a huge help in my plastic-free journey. Just because it is difficult, it doesn't mean that it isn't worthwhile. What is does mean, however, is that it will take some effort. You do have to change your lifestyle – quite dramatically, in fact – but this journal is here to help.

Rebecca Greig

THE PLASTIC PROBLEM

Begin your plastic-
free journey by
understanding why we
have to take notice

THE PLASTIC PROBLEM

> **Plastic waste is choking the planet and seriously harming marine life. What can we do to remove and prevent the waste from saturating the oceans?**

Somewhere between Hawaii and California, a vast inflatable coastline sweeps through the sea. Beneath a 600-metre-long float, a three-metre deep skirt rakes the ocean. Forced along by wind and waves, it moves faster than the currents, bending as it travels to form a U-shaped net. Fish dive beneath to escape its advances, but as the system roams the water it gathers a strange catch. Braving gales and storms and resisting the corrosive effects of sea salt, System 001 sends signals to satellites overhead and boats close by to collect a haul unlike any other. This net is trawling the great Pacific Garbage Patch, and its job is to clean up the sea.

The Pacific garbage patch

The Pacific Garbage Patch is a trash vortex; a swirling gyre of waste caught up in ocean currents. While not the literal island of rubbish sometimes described in the media, its waters are strewn with small chunks of floating debris. Churned by the action of the waves, the pieces bob up and down in the water column, circulating with the currents. Invasive species hitch a ride on the travelling plastics, making their way to waters nature never intended for their occupation. Sea birds, marine mammals and fish mistake the floating chunks for food, filling their bellies with indigestible trash. The pieces that remain wear away under the relentless rocking, rubbing microscopic plastic splinters and toxic chemicals into the water.

Deployed on 16 October 2018, System 001 aims to clear half of the rubbish from the Pacific Garbage Patch over the next five years. It is the first of a network of 60, and the result of more than 270 scale model tests and six prototypes. Pushed along by natural forces and equipped with solar-powered electronics, System 001 quietly follows the flow of the water. It's got lights and GPS to warn sailors, and it moves slowly enough that fish have plenty of time to get out of the way. Plastic, on the other hand, can't escape: trapped between the

> *"We waste 1 million plastic bottles a minute, half a million plastic straws a day and 4 trillion plastic bags every year"*

inflatable float and the solid skirt, it has nowhere to go. Load by load, sea-going rubbish trucks will retrieve the waste and start to clear the ocean. If all goes well, the project could roll out across the globe to remove 90 per cent of our floating junk by 2040.

How did we get here?

It's barely more than 100 years since Leo Baekeland invented the first fully synthetic plastic. Developed to insulate electrical wires at the tail end of the second industrial revolution, this new material was unlike anything seen before. Cheap to produce, resistant to heat and highly mouldable, it could be anything people wanted it to be, and its appearance kick-started a wave of chemical innovation.

All plastics have the same basic structure. Zoom in and most look like strings of pearls, with long, repeating chains that melt when they heat up and set hard as they cool. What makes them special is their versatility. We can extrude them into thin sheets, press them between rollers, blow them into bubbles, cast them like metal or vacuum mould them into 3D shapes. Changing the chemical building blocks of the chains can alter their flexibility, melting point and ability to resist chemicals. Additives between the chains can change their colour, make them fire-proof or kill bacteria, and adding branches to the chains can make them tangle, forming knots that don't melt and locking finished plastics into permanent shapes.

These incredible materials are cheap, clean and waterproof. They can be thick or thin, bendy or brittle, brightly coloured or completely clear. We can wear them against our skin, wrap them around our food and use them to construct everything from pens and tinsel to smartphones and spaceships. Plastics are strong enough to support buildings, light enough to fly and slippery enough to stop eggs sticking to frying pans. But these wonder materials are so cheap that we don't think twice about throwing them away. Today, we make 300 million tons of plastic a year, half of which goes straight in the bin. We waste 1 million plastic bottles a minute, half a million plastic straws a day and 4 trillion plastic bags every year. Of all the plastic we have ever made, nearly 80 per cent is in landfill or littering the natural world. Nearly a third of plastic packaging goes

What is plastic?

Plastic polymers are long chains of molecules linked by carbon-carbon bonds.

———————

Polymer chains contain thousands of repeating subunits called monomers.

———————

Polymers also exist in nature, but their chemical bonds break down more easily.

———————

Thermo- plastics melt when they get hot, reforming into new shapes.

———————

Thermosets fix into one shape and don't melt when heated.

———————

Chemical additives, like dyes, can slot between the polymer chains.

———————

There are seven kinds of plastic, sorted according to their chemical similarities.

———————

The raw ingredients for plastics are hydro-carbons from coal, gas and oil.

HOW DOES PLASTIC GET INTO THE ENVIRONMENT?

CONSTANT CONSUMPTION

The world produces 300 million tons of plastic each year, half of which we use just once before discarding it.

IN THE LAUNDRY

Acrylic clothes release over 700,000 plastic fibres per 6kg wash. Polyester releases nearly 500,000.

MICROPLASTIC SOUP

There are more than 5 trillion pieces of plastic floating about in the oceans.

CONTAMINATED WATER

Over 110,000 tons of microplastics wash over agricultural land in North America and Europe every single year.

PLASTIC PER PERSON

The average person in the EU makes around 31kg of plastic waste every year.

31 KG

RIVERS OF RUBBISH

Our rivers carry around 100,000 rubbish trucks' worth of plastic waste out to sea each year.

"We waste 1 million plastic bottles a minute, half a million plastic straws a day and 4 trillion plastic bags every year"

straight out to sea, where it will stay for several human lifetimes; enzymes made by living things can't touch the human-made chains that make plastic so strong and durable.

What can we do?

The Ocean Cleanup project sits at the very end of the plastic economy, mopping up the river of waste pouring out of our homes and businesses. But, as System 001 scours the sea, people across the globe are stepping up to battle the plastic production line.

The biggest plastic-producing sector is packaging. There are bags, trays and films made from low-density polyethylene (LDPE); milk and shampoo bottles made from high-density polyethylene (HDPE); water bottles and cleaning fluid bottles made from polyethylene terephthalate (PET); plates, cups and cutlery made from polystyrene; insulated packaging made from expanded polystyrene; and bottle caps, crisp packets and ice cream tubs made from polypropylene. Across the world, we use an estimated 10 million plastic bags every single minute. To stem the plastic tide, it makes sense to start here.

Since it launched in 2017, more than 50 countries have signed up to the UN Environment Clean Seas campaign. Single-use plastic is now firmly in the firing line, and countries across the world are phasing them out. Taiwan is ramping up to a total ban on single-use straws, cups and plastic bags, Zimbabwe plans to ban expanded plastic food packaging, and Kenya has already made plastic bags illegal; people found making, selling or using them face a fine of up to £30,000 (approximately $38,000) or up to four years in prison. They may seem drastic, but these tactics are working. In the UK, a 5p tax on single-use plastic bags has seen the number of bags used in England drop by more than 80 per cent.

Bags, straws and microbeads are some of the easiest targets; switching to non-plastic alternatives is cheap and simple. But when it

In Europe, a goal set in December 2017 aims to see

55%

of plastic packaging recycled by 2030.

> *"Scientists are experimenting with biodegradable plastics, like polylactide (PLA). It's made from lactic acid, which comes from corn"*

comes to other single-use products like bottles, cutlery and coffee cups, the challenge is greater. One option is to replace plastics with traditional materials. We could use glass, metal, paper, card or jute (vegetable fibre). Yet, while recyclable, these materials aren't always better for the environment. Making paper produces more pollution than making plastic, and it also consumes more energy and more water. And, while glass production is more environmentally friendly, the containers themselves are heavy and bulky, racking up more pollution when products are eventually shipped out.

Creative start-ups are already experimenting with new options, including cutlery made from wheat, water bottles made from seaweed and six-pack rings made from barley. Designed to disappear after you use them, they satisfy the craving for single-use solutions without polluting the planet. But knocking plastic off the top spot will take time. Until then, we need to work with what we've got.

In Japan, there are no plastic bans yet. Instead, they focus on waste management, prioritising recycling so that trash never reaches the sea. Non-recyclable plastics pass through incinerators, releasing heat that turns turbines to make electricity. This approach tries to turn our linear model of product design, consumption and waste into a more circular system. The dream would be to close the loop so that all discarded plastics become raw materials for future production. Changes to design and recycling could make products last longer, make them easier to repair and easier to repurpose at the end of their life, and changes to energy recovery methods could help us to get more out of plastics too contaminated for reuse.

This process is already underway. In Europe, a goal set in December 2017 aims to see 55 per cent of plastic packaging recycled by 2030. But there's only so much we can do in our own homes to recycle the goods we buy. To help us to achieve this goal, policy changes could start to make companies responsible for what happens to their products after

we've used them. In South Africa, for example, members of the PET Recycling Company pay a levy on the raw materials for plastic production. This money then goes back into redesigning packaging and recycling post-consumer waste. Not only does this help the planet, it also creates jobs, which can be better for economies than banning plastics all together. Back in the UK, the UK Plastics Pact is working with the packaging sector to transition to reusable, recyclable or compostable plastics. They also want to bring plastic recycling to 70 per cent by 2025.

Scientists are experimenting with biodegradable plastics, like polylactide (PLA). It's made from lactic acid, which comes from corn, and it takes just 12 months to break down. For plastics that we can't recycle, new methods hope to capture more energy from waste by turning them into fuels. A process called gasification heats plastics with air to make a gas that can be burnt. Another, called pyrolysis, heats them without air to make a liquid fuel like oil.

There are still problems to iron out with these new technologies. Burning plastic waste can be hazardous, and to make enough biodegradable plastics to replace the real thing we would need to turn over vast areas of land to corn monocultures. Then there is the fact that even though biodegradable plastics can break down, it doesn't mean that they will. They need to reach temperatures over 50 degrees Celsius, which is achievable inside industrial composters, but not when plastics escape into the ocean. But we're moving in the right direction, and we all have a part to play.

We as individuals can choose alternatives to plastics and put pressure on governments and brands to make bigger changes. If we focus on reduction, reuse and recycling, we could close the loop in the plastic economy and stop this incredible material leaking out into the sea.

How long does waste take to break down?

It is quite shocking when we look at how certain every day items that often end up in landfil take to fully decompose

2 months
To get rid of a cardboard box

1 month
For a paper bag to decompose

1 million years
For an aluminium can to break apart

2 years
To compost an orange peel

CIGARETTES

12 years
For a cigarette butt to disintegrate

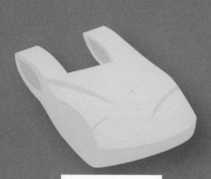

20 years
Until a plastic bag breaks apart

DRINK

Cola

450 years
For a plastic bottle to fall to bits

Approximately 5,000 items of marine plastic pollution have been found per mile of beach in the UK

ocean
IN NUMBERS

275 million METRIC TONS OF PLASTIC WASTE WAS MADE IN 2010 ALONE

MOST OF THE PIECES OF PLASTIC IN THE OCEAN MEASURE LESS THAN 5MM (0.2IN)

5.25 trillion Estimated number of pieces of plastic currently floating in the ocean

98%
of the plastic
currently in the
ocean is thin film,
fishing line and
unidentifiable
fragments

**334,000
Pieces**
Amount
of plastic in every
square kilometre
of the Great
Pacific Garbage
Patch

**8
Million**
APPROXIMATE AMOUNT
OF PLASTIC IN TONS
GOING INTO THE
OCEAN EVERY
SINGLE YEAR

2050
Scientists fear
that by 2050 there
will be more
plastic in the
ocean than
fish

Breaking the food chain

Plastics affect every level of
the marine ecosystem

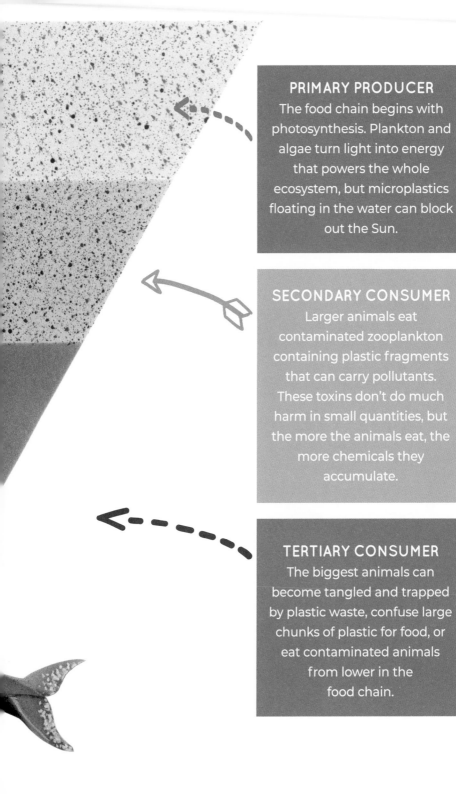

PRIMARY PRODUCER
The food chain begins with photosynthesis. Plankton and algae turn light into energy that powers the whole ecosystem, but microplastics floating in the water can block out the Sun.

SECONDARY CONSUMER
Larger animals eat contaminated zooplankton containing plastic fragments that can carry pollutants. These toxins don't do much harm in small quantities, but the more the animals eat, the more chemicals they accumulate.

TERTIARY CONSUMER
The biggest animals can become tangled and trapped by plastic waste, confuse large chunks of plastic for food, or eat contaminated animals from lower in the food chain.

THE WORST PLASTIC OFFENDERS

Plastic use is abundant in our society and there are different types of plastic that need to be handled in different ways. But do you know what they are?

*T*he reason plastics are such a popular material for making commodities is the same reason why plastic is a huge problem for the environment. It is incredibly tough. Depending on how plastic is treated it can withstand very high temperatures, will not be damaged by poor weather conditions, and will not deteriorate over time. Which is great when we need the products, but a real problem when we don't.

The time spent using a single-use plastic item, such as a drinking straw, coffee-cup lid, or soft drink bottle is a tiny fraction of the time that the same item is considered waste. A styrofoam cup, for example, can take between 50 and 500 years to break down in a rubbish dump, but will only be used for a single hot drink. This waste often disrupts the ecosystem, wherever it is left. Of course, we also use an abundance of plastic in our homes, and the issue of what happens after we have finished with the products that use them is no less a problem than single-use plastic items.

Know the type

Another factor is what type of plastic is being used. Some plastics can be safely reused in the home for years. Others, if treated improperly, can be dangerous in the home. For example, plastic is found in both microwave-safe food storage boxes and in foam containers for takeaway meals. The foam food containers are useful because they are resistant to heat, meaning they can be safely held. However, if a higher heat is directly applied to them (eg, in a microwave) toxic chemicals will leak out into the food.

Finally, some of these plastics may be recycled, so if you want to live in a sustainable way, knowing which ones can be recycled is just as important as knowing which of them can be used with food and drink. If it can't be recycled, it is important to consider how much you really need that particular brand of product when the time comes to replace it.

WHAT DO THE NUMBERS ON PLASTIC IN YOUR HOME MEAN?

There are many types of plastics commonly used in our households. These can be categorised by the 'resin identification code' on each item.

PETE/PET
(polyethylene terephthalate)

This type 1 plastic is used in water and fruit juice bottles, most soft drinks, cooking oil bottles, etc. These are considered single-use items, and repeated use can lead to leaching of carcinogens. These can be recycled into a number of useful items, so recycle them if you have the opportunity. It is important NOT to reuse them in the same manner.

HDPE
(high-density polyethylene)

This stiff type 2 plastic is used in milk bottles, cleaning products, shampoo/shower gel bottles. It is similar to PETE, but tougher. It is usually coloured, whereas PETE is usually transparent. As these products are high-density plastic, they will be accepted at most recycling centres. Unlike PETE, it can be reused to safely store food products.

PVC
(polyvinyl chloride)

Used in plastic packing, bubble wrap, pipes and coffee containers, PVC is a type 3 plastic and should be used carefully. If used incorrectly, chlorine and other chemicals can leak into food products, so only use it in the way the manufacturer suggests, particularly when it comes to foods. Items made of PVC will likely not be accepted for recycling.

LDPE
(low-density polyethylene)

Found in shopping bags, rubbish sacks and sandwich bags. These type 4 plastics are considered safe with food; however, they cannot be recycled easily, and it is possible recycling centres will not accept them. Cut down on LDPE by using reusable produce bags for loose items when shopping, as well as picking durable shopping bags.

"The time spent using a single-use plastic item is a fraction of the time that the same item is considered waste"

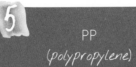

PP
(polypropylene)

A tough, lightweight plastic used in straws, toys, baby bottles, TVs, and food products such as microwavable containers. It has a high melting point, hence its safe use with foods. These can also be recycled, however only a small percentage of items containing PP ever are. Check with your local recycling centre to see if they will accept type 5 plastic items.

PS
(polystyrene)

A very versatile plastic used in toys, packaging, insulation and takeaway containers. Polystyrene is a type 6 plastic, is difficult to recycle and is damaging to the environment, as it is structurally weak. If possible, try and reduce the amount that you use this plastic, especially if you are only using it once. Do not ever directly heat polystyrene (eg, in a microwave).

OTHER PLASTICS
(nylon, fibreglass, acrylic, etc)

These are often a combination of types 1-6, and they are very hard to recycle for this reason. The best option for recycling is to send them back to the manufacturer. It's also important not to use them when using food (eg, microwave containers), as it is not possible to know what is in them.

Over

150

plastic bottles litter each mile of UK beaches.

5 HIDDEN PLASTICS FOUND LURKING IN SURPRISING PLACES

It's overwhelming to learn that plastic is lurking in some of the most unusual suspects. But were you aware of just how omnipresent plastic can really be?

COFFEE CUPS

The average disposable coffee cup is lined with a thin layer of plastic, designed to make it heat and leakproof. Unfortunately is also makes it increasingly difficult for them to be recycled.

TEA BAGS

Remarkably, plastic is found in tea bags! Polypropylene is added to the paper tea bag to heat seal them, which helps during manufacturing and also helps to prevent the bag from splitting in your cup.

WET WIPES

There is no denying how useful wet wipes are, but in terms of the environment they are doing more harm than good and they are full of microplastics. The bigger problem is that many people still flush wipes down the toilet.

CLOTHING

A lot of our clothes are made from plastic. Some of the key contenders are polyester, nylon, acrylic and other synthetic fibres. All release small microplastics when we wash our clothes and in turn end up in our waterways.

CHEWING GUM

Chewing gum is made from a polymer as opposed to the tree sap it used to be made out of. This makes it more durable and enables us to chew it for longer. However, it's awful for the environment as it doesn't biodegrade.

RECYCLING SYMBOLS

A universal language, recycling symbols tell us which bin to put our rubbish in – but do you know what they mean? Take a look at our handy guide below

MOBIUS LOOP

The Mobius Loop was arguably the most common and widely recognised recycling symbol in the world. Created for an art competition to celebrate the first Earth Day in 1970, the symbol is usually depicted in black, green or as an outline. The symbol means the item can be recycled, as opposed to being made of recycled materials.

Widely Recycled

WIDELY RECYCLED

This means the packaging can be recycled by more than 75% of local authorities in the UK. Sometimes other instructions are included, such as 'Rinse' (to reduce the risk of attracting vermin), 'Lid/Cap on' (to stop small parts falling through holes during the sorting process), 'Flatten' (to reduce space), and 'Remove Sleeve' (if it's not recyclable).

Check Locally

CHECK LOCALLY

The white circular arrow (same as above) on a black square means that only 20% to 70% of local authorities in the UK are equipped to recycle this form of material, usually a type of plastic. In this case it's best to look on your local council's website or contact the waste department for clarification.

Not Yet Recycled

NOT YET RECYCLED

Disappointingly this logo (which is the same as 'Check Locally' but with a diagonal line crossed through it), means the product is currently only recycled by fewer than 20% of local authorities in the UK. This symbol often appears on items like foil wrapping paper, bouquet film and crisp packets.

350 million tonnes of plastic are being produced each year. This could weigh more than humanity itself estimated at 316 million tonnes in 2013.

THE GREEN DOT

Commonly thought to mean the item is recyclable, this logo, showing two interlocking arrows that form a circle (sometimes in black and white, other times in light and dark green), actually means the manufacturer has paid a financial contribution to recycling services in Europe and isn't necessarily recyclable or made of recycled materials.

GLASS

This illustration, showing a person popping a bottle into a vestibule surrounded by a three-arrow triangle, explains that the packaging (usually a jar or bottle) is made of glass and should be disposed of at a bottle bank – remembering to separate colours, of course – or to use your council's household glass collection service.

RECYCLABLE ALUMINUM

This logo means the item is made of recycled aluminum. As well as foil, you'll find it on drink cans, screw-top lids, takeaway containers and roasting trays. If you're presented with a shiny wrapper and can't find the logo just scrunch it into a ball – if it stays scrunched it's aluminum foil, if it springs open it's not.

80% OF OCEAN PLASTIC COMES FROM LAND-BASED SOURCES

MY PLASTIC NOW

Think about why you want to go plastic free. Writing about why you are passionate about a cause into your own words can help you to really understand what makes it so important to you. Be honest about the plastic that you use now and hopefully you'll see a drastic change by the end of your journey.

Why have you chosen to go plastic free?

....
....
....
....
....
....
....
....
....

In your own words, what do you think are the biggest plastic problems?

....
....
....
....
....
....
....
....
....
....
....
....
....
....
....
....
....
....
....

What do you do that produces the most plastic?

....
....
....
....
....
....
....
....
....
....
....
....
....
....
....
....
....
....
....

Write down all of the cleaning products that you use that have plastic packaging.

1 ....
2 ....
3 ....
4 ....
5 ....
6 ....
7 ....
8 ....
9 ....
10 ....
11 ....
12 ....
13 ....
14 ....
15 ....
16 ....
17 ....
18 ....
19 ....
20 ....

Write down all of the beauty products that you use that have plastic packaging.

1	16
2	17
3	18
4	19
5	20
6	21
7	22
8	23
9	24
10	25
11	26
12	27
13	28
14	29
15	30

Bamboo brush

Bar of soap

Look at your kitchen and eating habits. Write down all of the plastic that you produce from food.

Plastic found	Times found in one week

WHAT DO WE NEED TO DO TOGETHER?

Plastic is a world-wide problem. While it's important to tackle it as individuals, it is vital that we also work together to make the biggest impact

lastics are part of so many of the things we use on a daily basis, and we have become so accustomed to its presence in our world, that it's hard to imagine life without it. It is useful because it is so durable compared to other materials, which makes disposing of the plastic a concern most manufacturers rather not worry about. As a species, we are also constantly making more plastic. In 1995, 156 million tons of plastic was being produced a year. Twenty years later that had more than doubled to 381 million tons, and there is little to indicate that the rate of growth is slowing. This would be less of an issue if we were recycling all of the plastic we are producing, but unfortunately only 9 per cent of the plastic produced has been recycled. As a best estimate, 5 billion tons of plastic (roughly equivalent to Manhattan, New York) has been discarded over the last hundred years.

How much plastic does one person produce?

Of course, it will depend on the lifestyle that they are living, but a person in North America or Europe will use an estimated 100 kg of plastic over the course of a single year. That is based on current usages of plastic, but as we have already mentioned, the amount of plastic that is produced each year is always growing, therefore unless we adopt a new attitude, that 100 kg annual usage will more than likely increase as time goes on, not decrease!

How can you have an impact?

So what steps can you, as one person, take to have a positive impact on the environment? There is a surprising amount that we can do as individuals to combat the problem. First, you are already making yourself aware of the issues and looking for a way to reduce plastic use by reading these pages. That's a fantastic start!

*"As with all big challenges in our
planet's history, the most effective way
of solving them is to work as a group"*

Make a plan of action

Consider how much plastic you will use from now on, and what you plan to do with the plastic when you're finished with it. There are various ways you can do this (journals, like this one, online blogs, 'plastic-use' calculators) and by doing so you'll have an idea of exactly how much plastic you use daily without really thinking about it. This will also be crucial in identifying where you can make changes to reduce the plastic that you are using.

Be proactive

Third, begin to make positive changes to actively use less plastic. Begin by refusing single-use plastic items if you don't need them, like straws or coffee stirrers. Bring reusable water bottles and hot drink mugs with you when you go out, and make sure you have a supply of reusable bags when you are about to do the weekly shop. If you occasionally forget, don't give yourself any grief for it – just make a plan that ensures you don't forget next time! As you get more conscientious about your plastic habits, you can examine other methods, such as looking for plastic-free options in local supermarkets, or only buying plastic products that can be easily recycled.

Changing the destructive effect of plastic on the environment might seem like too big a challenge for any one person to take on alone, and there is no reason why you should do so. There will be many other people in your community who have the same concerns as you, and by working together you'll be able to have a bigger impact, as well as encourage more people to join in the effort. As with all big challenges in our planet's history, the most effective way of solving them is to work as a group.

Find out if there is a campaign in your local area, and if there is, join it. This will enable you to pool resources and increase your own knowledge of what is already happening in your community. If there isn't a local campaign, try and find one online. There are people all over the world who care about this issue, so connect with them! Finally, if there isn't a campaign in your area, why don't you start one yourself?!

USE PLASTIC RESPONSIBLY

A good way of doing this is to keep a journal of the plastic items you are offered when out and about. For example, if you buy a sandwich in a plastic container, can you see a recycling point nearby? If not, are you able to hang onto the container until it can be recycled?

MAKE ENVIRONMENTALLY-FRIENDLY CHOICES!

Choose clothing and other products that do not use plastic microfibres (unless they have already been recycled), and support sustainable brands in your local community. Buying second-hand clothing brings considerable benefits to the environment in a number of ways (reducing packaging, production, carbon footprint in transportation). Finally, make sure you carry the following with you when you go out: reusable coffee cup, cutlery, reusable water bottle (glass/metal), cloth bag, reusable straw/stirrer. If you are going somewhere for dinner and expect leftovers, then why not bring a reusable container with you?

RECYCLE YOUR CLOTHES!

Plastic microfibres are found in a lot of clothes, especially T-shirts. Rather than throwing them away, give to charity shops, sell online or at vintage fairs, or pass on to friends. T-shirts can even be converted into shopping bags with a small amount of sewing! Look for other ways in which you can recycle old clothes online.

5
TIPS FOR BUILDING A PLASTIC-FREE CAMPAIGN IN YOUR COMMUNITY OR WORKPLACE

BUILD YOUR PLASTIC-FREE COLLECTIVE

Whether in your neighbourhood or workplace, advertise that you are going to form a plastic-free collective.

KNOW YOUR LOCAL RECYCLING POINTS

Where can you recycle easily? Do you have a weekly collection from your home, and is the bin big enough for all your recyclables? Do you know where the nearest centre is?

START SOME PLASTIC-FREE EVENTS LOCALLY

Raise awareness in your area by hosting plastic-free meals, where all of the ingredients are bought without plastic packaging!

LOBBY LOCAL BUSINESSES AND POLITICIANS FOR CHANGE

Engage with your local councils and businesses to let them know you are concerned about plastic waste. Once they know you care about your planet, they will feel incentivised to make a bigger effort.

REACH OUT TO OTHER GROUPS

Make sure you are all working towards similar goals and share information. They'll have good ideas you can try, and vice versa. The more people are involved on a national scale, the quicker awareness will grow.

Every day approximately **8** million pieces of plastic pollution find their way into our oceans

My plastic-free pledge

Starting today I pledge to go as plastic free as possible.

I pledge to...

- Refuse plastic whenever I can. Such as not using plastic straws, bags, coffee cups, bottles or any other single use product.

- **Reduce my plastic footprint by opting for non-plastic sturdy materials.**

- Reuse and repurpose plastic items like containers where I was unable to avoid them.

- **Ensure unavoidable plastic is recycled in the correct way**

- Spread the word and tell everyone I know about what I am doing and encourage them to join me.

- **Hold companies accountable for their plastic use and campaign for change.**

Signed: _____   **Date:** _____

PLASTIC-
FREE FOOD

Food related plastic
is one if the worst
offenders, let's take a
look at what we can do

THE FOOD AND DRINK PROBLEM

Even just picking up a few bits in your local supermarket can result in a deluge of unwanted plastic waste. Here are some steps you can take to avoid this as much as possible

t's not an unusual to come home from your weekly food shop and be surrounded by single-use plastic as you unpack your shopping bags. Almost everything we purchase from our local supermarket is surrounded in the stuff. Arguably the problem stems from manufacturers and supermarkets not offering alternatives to consumers in the first place. Experts believe that UK supermarkets are producing 810,000 tonnes of single-use plastic every year. However, there is an argument that plastic food packaging does serve a purpose. Most of the time it helps protect food while in transit, making it last longer and minimising food waste. By the time the plastic reaches our homes, many of us will recycle but it may be shocking to learn that only 9 per cent of the world's plastic is recycled. Given that statistic, we need to be trying to avoid plastic in our food shop altogether. But how easy is this?

What are supermarkets doing about it?

The good news is that the plastic problem is well reported in the media, making it impossible for many big supermarkets to ignore it. In the UK, many supermarkets have addressed the problem head on with the likes of Waitrose, Lidl and Tesco adopting many plastic-free plans that include plastic bottle deposit schemes and ending the sale of plastic bags. Across the

MAKE AN ECOBRICK

One way to use some of the unnecessary plastic packaging that comes with our food and drink consumption is to make an ecobrick. An ecobrick can be used as a building block and is created by filling a plastic bottle with clean, dry plastic that becomes tightly packed to form a brick.

"A way to avoid the plastic waste created by supermarkets is by choosing to shop at your local farmers' market"

pond in the US, Trader Joe's has promised to reduce plastic by 500 tons in 2019 and Kroger suggests it will stop giving out plastic bags. If you do opt for shopping in large supermarkets then one of the easiest steps to reduce your plastic waste is to reuse your shopping bags. Since the 5p charge on plastic bags was brought in to the UK in 2015, sales of bags have dropped by 86 per cent – a staggering statistic given our previous addiction to them.

What can you do?

Waste-free supermarkets and local shops are popping up all over the place. One way to reduce your plastic waste is by supporting these small independent companies that are passionate about plastic pollution. Most of these shops have dedicated refill zones designed for stocking up on groceries and dry goods without the need for single-use containers. Another way to avoid the plastic waste created by supermarkets is by choosing to shop at your local farmers' market. Most cities across the world have residential markets where you can buy cheap local produce. Not only is this good for the local economy as it supports farmers, but it also avoids unnecessary packaging used in transit.

RECYCLE	WAITROSE WASTE
When plastic packaging can't be avoided, it's important to try and recycle where possible. But it's important to know what you can and can't recycle. One of the best ways to do this is by checking with your local council. Once you are aware of what you can recycle, then make sure it is rinsed and disposed of.	In June 2019, Waitrose UK trialled its first waste-free shopping experience. The shop in Oxford offered over 200 loose lines to shoppers, including pasta, lentils and cleaning products. Waitrose has also signed up to the UK Plastic Pact and is committed to offering a choice of 160 loose fruit and vegetables.

WRITE A SHOPPING LIST

Sit down and make a list of what you buy now and
what the plastic-free alternative would be. Then
you can slowly make the swap to a plastic-free life!

What I buy now	Plastic-free alternative

TIPS FOR PLASTIC-FREE FOOD SHOPPING

Follow this handy advice to avoid unnecessary plastic when you are on your next food shop

BRING YOUR OWN BAGS

Make sure you are always prepared by carrying around a couple of reusable bags either in your rucksack/ handbag or in the boot of your car.

BUY LOOSE FRUIT AND VEG

Some supermarkets offer vegetables and fruit that are sold separately, like peppers. Try and buy these instead of multipacks.

THINK TWICE

We are lucky enough to be surrounded by choice. Instead of reaching for products in plastic, try switching to glass or tin.

DON'T PANIC

Forgotten your reusable bags? Don't worry! Often supermarkets will have boxes from deliveries stacked somewhere. Instead of buying another bag, just pack your shopping in a box instead.

USE WASTE-FREE SHOPS

Fill up on all of the bare essentials at your local waste-free shop. Make sure you remember to take containers, reusable bags or glass jars to stock up on the everyday necessities like rice and oats.

MAKE YOUR OWN TEAS

It may surprise you to learn that plastic is in your everyday brew. The bag itself is fused together with a plastic polymer that holds the tea leaves inside and stops it falling apart in your mug. As an alternative, give some of these tea recipes a go to avoid those plastic nasties.

Fresh Moroccan mint

Ingredients

- Handful fresh mint leaves
- 1 tsp brown sugar

1. **Boil the kettle.**
2. Break a handful of leaves in the palm of your hand to release the oils of the mint.
3. **Drop leaves into a mug.**
4. Stir in the sugar and allow to dissolve.

Lemon & Ginger

Ingredients

- 2-3cm fresh ginger
- 2-3 slices of lemon

1. **Boil the kettle.**
2. Thinly slice the lemon and chop the ginger, ensuring to remove the outer skin.
3. **Place in a mug and pour in the hot water.**
4. Leave to stand for 3 minutes.

Masala chai

Ingredients

- 1 ½ cups | 350 ml milk or dairy free alternative
- ½ tbsp loose leaf black tea
- 3 cracked cardamon pods
- ½ cinnamon stick or 1 tsp mixed spice
- 2 cloves
- 2 tsp soft brown sugar

1. **Heat the milk in a saucepan over a very low heat.**
2. Add tea, cracked cardamom pods, cinnamon, cloves and soft brown sugar.
3. **Leave on a gentle heat until it starts to boil and then remove from heat.** Strain and serve.

Cinnamon tea

Ingredients

- 1 cinnamon stick
- 1 tsp Assam leaf tea
- 1 tsp honey

1. **Bring 300ml of water to the boil with a cinnamon stick in it. Then remove from the heat and add the Assam tea leaves for 1-2 mins.**
2. Remove the cinnamon stick.
3. **Strain and serve wtih the teaspoon of honey.**

AVOID LOTS OF PACKAGING

Avoid all of the unnecessary packaging that comes with shop-bought food with these hearty homemade recipes. Share them with your friends and family and get them on board too!

Make your own granola

Ingredients

- 2 tbsp coconut oil
- ½ cup | 125 ml maple syrup
- 2 tbsp honey (substitute for extra maple syrup for vegan alternative)
- 1 tsp vanilla extract
- 3 cups | 300 g rolled oats
- ¾ cup | 100 g of seeds (sunflower, pumpkin or sesame seeds)
- ¾ cup | 100 g flaked almonds
- ½ cup | 50 g raisins
- ½ cup | 50 g cranberries

1. **Preheat oven to 150°C/300°F/Gas 2.**
2. Mix the coconut oil, maple syrup, honey and vanilla in a large mixing bowl and combine the remaining ingredients – leaving the dried fruit aside.
3. **Tip the granola onto two baking sheets, spread evenly and bake for 15 minutes.**
4. Allow to cool then add the dried fruit.

Blackcurrant squash

Ingredients

- 1 ½ cup | 300g golden caster sugar
- Zest and juice of 2 lemons
- 5 cups | 500g blackcurrants

1. **Place the sugar along with 1 cup |300ml of water in a pan.**
2. Bring to a simmer and then add the blackcurrants and the lemons.
3. **Once the blackcurrants have softened, remove from the heat and sieve through into a jug.**
4. Serve diluted with either tap water or sparkling water.

Make your own crisps

Ingredients

- 4 cups | 240g washed kale
- Salt and pepper
- 2 tbsp olive oil

1. **Preheat the oven to 150°C/300°F/ Gas 2.**

2. Toss the kale in a bowl with a light coating of olive oil and season with salt and pepper.

3. **Transfer to two baking trays, making sure that the kale is evenly distributed.**

4. Bake for 15 minutes or until crisp.

5. **Remove from the oven and serve immediately or transfer to an airtight container.**

Make your own dairy-free milk

Ingredients

- 2 cups | 200g rolled oats
- 4 cups | 1 litre water
- 1-2 dates or tbsp maple syrup

1. **Add the oats, water and dates to a blender and whiz for 30-45 seconds.**

2. Remove from the blender and pour the mixture over a large mixing bowl covered with a very thin towel or a clean T-shirt.

3. **Repeat this action of straining twice. Place into a jug and chill in the fridge.**

MAKE YOUR OWN SOUPS

There is nothing more comforting than a wholesome bowl of soup – especially when it avoids plastic containers!

Sweet potato and red lentil

Ingredients

- 2 tsp cumin
- 1 onion
- 2 garlic cloves
- 2 cups |400g sweet potatoes
- 1 ltr veg stock
- ¼ cup | 60 g red lentils
- Handful coriander leaves

1. **Finely dice the onion and fry on a low to moderate heat along with the garlic and cumin.**

2. Meanwhile, peel and chop the sweet potatoes and tip into the pan along with the stock and lentils.

3. **Bring to the boil and simmer for 20 mins.**

4. Blend until smooth using a stick blender and serve with a handful of coriander.

Spicy root veg

Ingredients

- 2 onions
- 2 sweet potatoes
- 2 carrots
- 2 parsnips
- ¼ cup | 50g green lentils
- 1 tbsp ground cumin
- 1 tsp chilli flakes
- 1 ltr vegetable stock
- 1 tbsp olive oil
- 2 cloves garlic

1. **Preheat oven to 200C/400F/ gas 6.**

2. Chop the veg and place on a baking tray. Drizzle with olive oil and sprinkle with cumin, chilli flakes and garlic.

3. **Roast for 30 minutes.**

4. Once the vegetables have softened add to a saucepan of stock along with the lentils.

5. **Bring to the boil and simmer for 20 minutes. Blend until smooth.**

Leek & potato

Ingredients

- 1 onion
- 1½ cups | 400g chopped potatoes
- 4 cups | 400g leeks (whites only)
- 1 ltr vegetable stock
- 140ml single cream (or vegan cream for dairy-free alternative)
- 1 clove garlic

1. **Dice the onion and fry on a low to moderate heat along with the garlic.**
2. Once the onions have softened, add the chopped potatoes, leeks and the vegetable stock. Bring to the boil and simmer.
3. **Remove from the heat and blend until super smooth.**
4. Slowly stir in the cream, then taste and adjust the seasoning accordingly.

Mushroom

Ingredients

- 2 medium onions
- 1 clove garlic
- 7 cups | 500g mushrooms
- 2 tbsp plain flour
- 1 ltr vegetable stock
- 4 tbsp single cream

1. **Cook the diced onions and garlic until soft. Add mushrooms and cook over a high heat for another 3 minutes until softened.**
2. Sprinkle over the flour and stir to combine.
3. **Pour in the vegetable stock.**
4. Bring the mixture to the boil and simmer for around 20 minutes.
5. **Remove from the heat and blitz using a hand blender until smooth. Return to the stove on a low heat and stir in the cream.**

STORE YOUR FOOD WITHOUT PLASTIC

From appliances to plastic wrap, Tupperware and party paraphernalia, the kitchen is littered with plastic. However, there are many ways to make a change...

 ost kitchens are packed to the rafters with plastic. By swapping these items for alternatives that are made of natural, yet sustainably sourced and reusable materials, you can relax knowing that you're not only doing your bit for the planet but looking after your health too, as some plastics have been found to contain BPA. Apart from these problematic plastic items you don't necessarily need to have to a mass cull – the next time you make a purchase, just question whether there is a better, more environmentally-friendly alternative out there. Here are just a few to get you started...

Cheerio plastic wrap

When it comes to covering food, most of us reach for the plastic wrap. However, this can't be recycled and will only end up in a landfill, so it's worth exploring some other options. One of the easiest is to put your foodstuff on a plate and cover with an upturned bowl. Alternatively you could reuse an unwanted, clean shower cap, like the ones provided in a hotel room. Yes, they are plastic but if you already own one and are thinking of binning it, this is a great way to repurpose it because the elasticated hem hugs around the sides of bowls and cups, plus it can be rinsed and reused. Unbleached baking paper, which can be recycled, or

AVOID THE BUGS

Buying in bulk from the whole food shop is a great idea but you have no idea if the food has picked up pests such as weevils. Weevils are small beetles that munch on grains, rice, nuts and other cereals. One way to get rid of them is to pop the food in a freezable container and leave in the freezer for at least two days.

foil, which can be washed, reused and eventually recycled, are other viable non-plastic options to consider.

Food to go

There's no shortage of choice when it comes to grabbing food or drink on the go, but with more choice comes higher waste, as much of the packaging can't be recycled. A 2018 report from the Environmental Audit Committee found that in the UK alone, 7 million disposable coffee cups are used every day, equating to 2.5 billion every year, creating concern that generated the so-called 25p 'latte levy' on disposable cups and a call for all takeaway cups to be made recyclable by 2023. Due to problems with most takeaway cups' engineering, they can't currently be widely recycled – the committee discovered less than 1% of all coffee cups are actually recycled. And it's not just hot drinks that are an issue, with the organisation Earth Day reporting that 1 million plastic bottles are bought every minute, of which it's estimated less than a quarter are recycled. The solution is simple, buy a reusable bottle anc fill up at home or from one of the growing

PARTY-TIME ALTERNATIVES TO PLASTICS

When it comes to entertaining, put down the single-use plastic plates, cups and cutlery. Where possible use your normal crockery and cutlery; every party has a volunteer that will help clean up, and if you have a dishwasher then really there's no excuse. If you don't have enough of something, just ask to borrow some from a friend. If the venue is away from home, or you've planned a picnic, there are still plenty of environmentally-friendly options. Try reusable items such as those made from silicone or get fancy with trendy bamboo sets that are perfect for picnicking for years to come. If it's high volume you need, recyclable wooden pieces may be the only answer. Just ensure they carry the widely recycled symbol before you buy.

number of public water supplies. For hot drinks, take your own portable mug to the cafe and benefit from varying incentives, such as money off or extra reward points. For food, consider dining in eateries that use recyclable or compostable packaging, or make something at home and pack it up in a stainless steel or sustainably sourced bamboo lunch box, or insulated canvas cool bag.

Say toodle-oo to Tupperware

Pyrex or ceramic dishes with lids or stainless steel tins – which will survive the oven and the freezer – are versatile Tupperware replacements. Silicone is another alternative. Commonly misconceived to be a plastic, silicone is actually part of the rubber family. Lightweight, easy to clean and relatively inexpensive, there are many silicone products on the market, including Joie Fresh Stretch Silicone pods, which are specifically shaped containers for food items.

As well as storage, think about all plastic items found in your kitchen, be it utensils, plates, bowls or cups. When it comes to replacing them, aim for metal, wooden or ceramic substitutes. Start small and the changes will soon add up.

DON'T CLING TO THE PAST

Reusable food wraps (such as Bee's Wraps), are becoming an increasingly popular, natural and sustainable alternative to plastic wrap. Available in a range of different shapes and sizes, look for ones composed of natural fibres that are coated on one side with a natural substance like beeswax (which has the benefit of being naturally anti-bacterial) or tree resin, or a vegan alternative such as soy and candelilla wax. To use a wrap, fold it over on itself in the case of sandwiches or place it over a bowl if storing food, then warm it slightly in your hands so the 'sticky' layer adheres to the desired surface. After use, wash in cool water with mild soap, leave to dry and reuse. What's more, at the end of its lifespan, which won't be for some time, it can be composted.

5

TOP OPTIONS FOR TUPPERWARE ALTERNATIVES

Stop relying on plastic to store your food and follow these simple tips

BOWL AND PLATE

An age-old trick passed down through the generations; nothing is simpler or more cost effective than turning a bowl over and placing it atop a plate of food to keep it fresh.

GO FOR GLASS

Glass jars with lockable lids, such as Kilner, are a super storage solution to keep food safe from pests and airtight for freshness. Alternatively, just recycle used jars, such as jam jars.

REPURPOSE OLD TUBS

Rather than buying new plastic containers,
save pennies as well as the environment
by reusing old takeaway containers,
ice cream tubs and biscuit tins to store your
food in.

MUSLIN BAGS

Muslin bags are breathable and therefore
perfect for storing (and separating),
fruits and vegetables. What's more, they're
super light and can easily be rolled up to
take to the shop with you.

COMPOST IS KING

As well as bowls, plates, cups and cutlery,
you can now also buy biodegradable storage
boxes that are suitable for both hot and cold
food. Then when you're ready to part with it,
just pop it on the compost heap!

STOP BUYING LUNCH ON THE GO

Buying lunch is convenient, but just think of all that single-use plastic! Try these easy-to-make bites instead. They can be made ahead of time and popped in a reusable tub, ready for lunch

A great Greek pasta

Ingredients

Serves 1

- 85g | 3oz pasta (penne or fusilli)
- Zest and juice of ½ lemon
- ¼ finely chopped red onion
- ¼ cucumber, cubed
- 4 cherry tomatoes, quartered
- Handful pitted black olives
- Handful of spinach
- 60g | 2 ¼ oz cubed feta
- Few basil leaves
- ½ tbsp olive oil

1. **Cook the pasta in salted boiling water for 12-14 minutes (depending on your preference).**

2. Blend the lemon, onion and oil together to make a dressing, adding pepper to season.

3. **Drain the pasta and place under cold running water.**

4. Stir the dressing over the washed and prepared salad, then mix with the pasta and feta cubes.

Grilled chicken and avocado sandwich

Ingredients

- 1 chicken breast
- ¼ courgette, thinly sliced
- ½ red or yellow pepper, thinly sliced
- ½ lemon, juiced
- ½ avocado, thinly sliced
- Handful of lettuce, thinly sliced
- Two slices of wholemeal bread or an individul baguette
- 1 tbsp natural yogurt
- Extra virgin olive oil

Serves 1

1. **Butterly the chicken breast by running your knife down the centre to flatten it out. Then fry or griddle flat for several minutes alternating sides until cooked through.**

2. Add the courgette and pepper cook for another 2 minutes. Remove everything from the heat, set aside, sprinkling on seasoning, lemon juice and oil.

3. **Take one slice of bread and layer on the yogurt, cooked veg, chicken, avocado and lettuce, then add the other slice of bread.**

Ham and cheese croissant

Ingredients

- 1 croissant
- 2 teaspoons dijon mustard
- 2 thin slices of ham
- 2 slices of mild cheese
- Few sprigs of watercress
- Optional pear, thinly sliced

Serves 1

1. **Cut the croissant horizontally and spread on the mustard.**

2. Layer the ham, cheese, watercress and pear (if desired) on the bottom half.

3. **Add a sprinkle of salt and pepper, then pop on the top half.**

Vegan chickpea and avocado salad

Ingredients

Serves 4

- 1 cup | 200 g dried quinoa
- 4 ½ cups | 735 g cooked chickpeas
- 80 ml water
- 2 tbsp lemon juice
- 1 ½ tbsp tahini
- 1 ½ tsp Dijon mustard
- ½ tsp salt
- Pepper, to taste
- ½ red onion, diced
- 30 cherry tomatoes, sliced
- ½ packed cup corriander (cilantro)
- 1 medium avocado, diced

1. **Rinse the quinoa in cold water then cook following the instructions on the packaging.**

2. Place ⅓ cup of chickpeas in a blender or food processor with the water, tahini, lemon juice, dijon, salt and pepper. Then blend until smooth and creamy.

3. **Toss all of the other ingredients in a bowl with the cooled quinoa and drizzle over with the creamy dressing.**

HEAD TO P178 FOR SPACE TO WRITE DOWN YOUR OWN RECIPES

WHAT'S THE PROBLEM WITH COFFEE CUPS?

Although largely made of cardboard, the problem with takeaway cups is the thin, almost invisible plastic polyethylene liner bonded to the inside of the cup so that it remains waterproof and doesn't fall apart when the beverage is added. Furthermore, as the cups have been 'contaminated' with drink, they can't be recycled at traditional plants and instead need to go to a specific recycling centre, of which only three exist in the UK.

STRAWS SUCK

Single-use plastic straws, once the staple of any good party, are slowly being phased out as news that they often escape refuse centres and fall into our waterways and seas, devastating marine life, has made people take notice. That said, the organisation Earth Day suggests half a million plastic straws are still used every day. To do your bit, opt for cardboard straws, which can be recycled, or the stainless steel variety, which are significantly more sturdy and reusable.

APPLY A NEW MINDSET TO APPLIANCES

While plastic kitchen appliances are often better for your wallet, they aren't necessarily better for your health, as many plastic-based machines (as well as food and beverage containers) are made using BPA. This plastic is favoured by manufacturers because it is strong and can cope with extremely high temperatures. However, issues arise when the toxic chemical enters the body, as research has linked it to neurological and reproductive problems, as well as Alzheimer's and cardiovascular disease. As a rule of thumb, if it doesn't say it's BPA-free, is microwave-safe, has a triangle with the number 3 (PVC) or 7 – it's a good idea to steer clear. Although this is easy to establish in the case of cups and bowls, it's harder to discern whether your kettle or coffee maker contains BPA, so consider a plastic-free alternative such as one made from stainless steel, or use glass jugs instead of plastic. The ways to minimise plastic consumption in the kitchen don't end there – for example when choosing your next coffee machine, consider opting for one that offers a coffee pod (capsule) recycling scheme, such as Nespresso.

SAVE OUR SPUDS

When it comes to storing root vegetables like potatoes and carrots – items that won't necessarily end up in your fridge's salad crisper – try an old-fashioned sack. There are many varieties available but look for one that is sturdy, flat bottomed, machine washable, and made from a breathable material that enables the air to circulate and stop your food 'sweating' and therefore rotting. Ideally plump for one that includes a liner to block out light and prevent the spuds turning green (showing a build up of toxins), such as the Lakeland Potato bag, which also features a trap door at the bottom to ensure the oldest veg comes out first. As well as potatoes, there are dozens of options for all types of vegetables in corresponding sizes and designs.

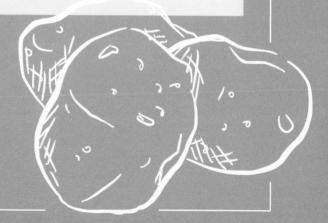

PLASTIC-FREE HOME

It's time to have a closer look at your own plastic use and how to change your ways

EVERY DAY PLASTIC FREE

We are living in a world where we are constantly in contact with plastic. But what can we do to break free from it in our day-to-day lives?

lastic creeps into our lives daily without us even being aware of it, and sadly we've become so accustomed to it that we don't even realise how much we rely on it. We are all aware of the usual plastic suspects – bottles, shower gels and coffee cups, for example – but have you considered other areas of your life where plastic is being repeatedly used and consumed?

One way that we can minimise the amount of plastic we are using is by altering our shopping habits and where we are purchasing from.

Go back to the high street

Many of us have turned to shopping online instead of on the high street. This is for many reasons, including its ease and the fact that it can be more cost-effective, but did you know that is one of the worst offenders when it comes to waste? Retailers almost always over-pack a product to ensure that goods arrive in perfect condition, which means that sometimes the smallest items are surrounded by excessive one-time-use packaging. These can range from plastic 'air-bags' to polystyrene – more often than not, both of these end up in landfill after we have received our order. So how can you prevent this? Simply minimise the number of items you buy online and, where possible, try to switch to shopping on the high street. If you must shop online then do a bit of research beforehand to see what materials retailers pack their products in.

Support companies that care

You should support companies that care about managing their waste. Lush is a great example of a company that has confronted the plastic problem head on. If packaging is unavoidable with one of their products, they make sure to use recycled materials. When it comes to packing orders, they also make sure that everything is wrapped with recycled paper and protected using Ecoflow, which is made from potato starch and is 100% biodegradable.

Be prepared

It isn't just about switching up our shopping habits – there are also other little changes you can make to reduce your amount of waste every day. Most of the time you can minimise your waste by just being prepared. For example, if you find yourself buying a takeaway coffee most mornings on your way to work, make sure you've got a reusable cup to hand. Not only are you reducing the need for a one-time-use coffee cup, but you might also save yourself some money as most places now offer a discount when you use your own cup.

While you're at it, try to avoid reaching for an easy meal deal on your lunch break because food-to-go generates an astonishing 11 billion items of packaging waste according to research from environmental charity Hubbub. Instead, make your own packed lunches and consider investing in reusable tupperware.

If you are someone who regularly goes out for post-work drinks, make sure you avoid plastic straws. One study published last year estimated that as many as 8.3 billion plastic straws pollute the world's beaches, and while plastic straws have been banned in the UK from 2020, bars will continue to stock them and will provide them if a customer requests one.

Stream your entertainment

But our daily plastic waste doesn't just stop at food and drink. As consumers we should also be more aware about how we engage with entertainment on a day-to-day basis. For example, instead of buying DVDs and CDs, consider signing up to online streaming services, such as Now TV, Netflix and Spotify. Watching and listening to movies, music and TV online reduces the amount of plastic CD and DVD cases that end up in landfill once we have become tired of a show or album. However, if you are someone who enjoys collecting DVDs and CDs, endeavour to buy them second hand from charity shops.

As consumers we have a choice of where to shop and what to buy, so it's important that we are mindful of our choices. Start by thinking about where you

do your food shop, what you are ordering online and how you are engaging with the entertainment industry and you'll be surprised at how a small change can be such a big step in the right direction.

Ultimately, if you want to reduce your plastic waste then preparation is the real key to success. Try to make a conscious effort to carry a reusable coffee cup or water bottle and make packed lunches. Most importantly, don't punish yourself too much if you slip up. We're all human and mistakes happen – just be sure that it doesn't become a regular habit!

YOUR ON-THE-GO WASTE

Make a note of all of the plastic items you come into contact over the space of a week. Now beside it, jot down how you are going to action this and prevent consuming that plastic waste.

Item	How many times used?	Future plan

THE PROBLEM WITH FAST FASHION

We have a love affair with fast fashion – and it's toxic. Read on to find out the devastating truth about our addiction to clothes and how it's destroying the environment

 e are addicted to clothes. It's not just shopping – we're addicted to making them. Many fashion companies, who used to only offer two collections a year, have now increased this up to 24 collections every single year. Not only is this incredibly taxing on the environment, with the fast-fashion industry responsible for producing over 20% of global wastewater, but it also contributes to the plastic problem. With their jazzy shop fronts, online deals and their low prices, the fast-fashion industry is a consumer's dream, but it's taking a huge toll on our planet and it's time we started acting on it.

Three weeks

This is the average amount of time that a piece of clothing will last in a wardrobe. With the meteoric rise of online shopping and the near-constant stream of new online retailers popping up, it's a tragic but unsurprising statistic. With the rise of social media, many are afraid of being photographed in the same outfit twice. This is where some of the biggest problems lie. When most people are finished with clothing they donate it to charity shops in the hopes of alleviating some of the guilt of one-wear fashion. However, if an item is left unsold at a charity shop then it's sent to landfill alongside other household waste – 73% of donated clothes end up in the bin.

CARBON FOOTPRINT

Global emissions from textile production equates to 1.2 billion tonnes of CO_2. A figure that is so high that it outweighs the international carbon footprint from flights and shipping combined. What's even sadder is to learn that from a Pulse report they have forecasted that these fashion emissions will grow by 63% by 2030.

The synthetic snake

Do you check your labels before you buy a new item of clothing? If you do, you have probably noticed that most clothes are made from a mixture of polyester, cotton and nylon. So, what's the problem with this? Polyester is a plastic – that's right, you are wearing plastic. We are all aware of the current plastic problem that our oceans are facing but what you may not be aware of is that fast fashion is actually contributing to this problem. In fact, a wash load of polyester clothes releases up to 70,000 microplastic fibres into our waterways. Sadly, half a million tons of these tiny microplastics are released into our sea each year, damaging ecosystems. The proportion of these synthetic fibres in our clothes has doubled since 2000 and has now risen to 60%. These fibres are made from oil, which is not not only bad for the environment – one polyester shirt has a 5.5kg carbon footprint – but it's also bad for your skin as you are essentially wearing petrol.

A rainbow of destruction

A clothing rail full of distinctive colours, and fantastic prints are all part of the appeal when it comes to shopping, but many of these features are achieved using toxic chemicals. After agriculture, textile dyeing is the second largest polluter of clean water. When these chemicals end up in the water system, those living in the surrounding areas end up drink this water, which can be carcinogenic and detrimental to human health.

THIRSTY WORK

Think you're being kinder to the planet and your wash load with your 100% cotton t-shirt? It's time to think again. It's true that avoiding synthetics like polyester will avoid tiny microplastics from finding their way into our oceans, but there is a price to pay for natural fabrics, too. The average amount of water used for a kilo of cotton, which in layman's terms can be a pair of jeans, is a staggering 10,000-20,000 litres.

THE INSIDE TRUTH

We spoke to Molly Board, who works for Jacobs Well
in India, about challenging the complexities of the
fast-fashion industry for the last century

Tell us a bit about yourself. Where are you currently working and who are 'Jacobs Well'?

I am a BA graduate of Fashion Design and Technology specialising in zero-waste pattern cutting and sustainability, currently living in Bangalore, India. I am working for a fair trade ethical production house in called Jacobs Well and I blooming love it.

Jacobs Well is different to your usual factory. For the last 20 years they have been offering education for young girls that have come from some of the poorest slums, orphanages and communities of India. Jacobs Well gives these women hope, a chance at a new life, independence and – most importantly – dignity. Here, these women learn everything from English to tailoring and receive support from a regular income. Whether you are an international company or an emerging independent designer, they can oversee a design from conception through to production.

Are most fast-fashion factories in Bangalore like this?

Sadly not, this is what makes Jacobs Well different to the usual production line. In other factories no fair wage is paid and often there are not enough man hours to meet the production demand. There is also no health and safety regulations in place, meaning that these women are working in dangerous conditions.

Can you keep 'on trend' and enjoy fashion but still be mindful of your consumption?

Yes, absolutely! The best thing about recycling and reusing your old clothes is that you can be creative. Instead of reaching for new items, why not try to wear your clothes in a different way? If you are looking for ways to use your summer clothes then try wearing long-sleeved tops under your summer dresses. This way you avoid having to invest in new clothes every change of season. Another thing to consider is having a capsule wardrobe with neutral colours. Investing and preserving clothes like this provides you with looks that will last you a lifetime and I can guarantee you'll always be on trend.

5

TIPS TO AVOID THE DESTRUCTIVE FAST FASHION INDUSTRY

Molly Board gives her advice for someone looking to minimise their impact on the environment through fashion

STOP CONSUMING

Consumerism is an evil cycle, but it's important to slow down your purchasing habits. You'll quickly realise you don't need any more. If you do find yourself shopping then make sure it's necessary.

SAVE

Stopping buying allows you to save so much more money. Instead of spending £20 a pop on cheap tops, you can finally invest it into something more important.

SHOP CHARITY

On the occasion you have the urge to shop,
immerse yourself in your local charity
shops instead of the high street.
Charity shops often have hidden gems lurking
on their shelves.

SHOP INDEPENDENT

Look for independent brands who can tell
you the name of their suppliers, where their
fabric was weaved, and who sewed their
garments. Do your research and shop around –
these brands exist!

CLOTHES SWAP

A great way of avoiding clothes waste is by
swap your clothes with your friends. Be
generous – if you hardly wear something and
they really love it just give it to them.

To learn more about Jacobs Well, check them
out on Instagram at @jacobswellindia

WHAT DO YOU NEED IN YOUR WARDROBE?

So many of us wake up in the morning and think: 'I have nothing to wear', when in fact our wardrobes are packed. Stop using this excuse to hit the high streets and instead embrace what you already have. Spend some time going through your wardrobe now and list items that need some attention or repairs. Use this time to also remove any unwanted plastic items. Remember to recyple the unwated clothing.

Item of clothing	Problem	Solution

RECYCLED CLOTHING

Spend some time researching upcoming vintage
clothes fairs and clothes swaps near you

Event name	Date	Location

MAKE YOUR BATHROOM MORE ECO

> It's hard to know where to start when it comes to embarking on a eco-friendly life but the good news is that the bathroom is one of the easiest places to begin

Our bathrooms amass a lot of waste – and no, we're not just talking about the natural kind! It doesn't take a lot to notice how quickly our bathroom bins fill up with rubbish. In the average household bin you are likely to find many re-occurring offenders from cotton buds to contact lenses and baby wipes. We are living in a world where most products are one-time use and we accumulate a lot of plastic waste because of this, which is having a devastating effect on many of our seaside towns and waterways. It can be overwhelming figuring out where to start, but the bathroom is a great place to begin reducing your plastic footprint. However, it isn't just plastic that is problem in our bathrooms – there are many repeat suspects that also have a detrimental effect on our planet.

Ditch the wipes

We have a huge addiction to wipes – in fact, we pretty much have a wipe for everything. Yes, they are super handy with their versatility and durability, from cleaning dirty babies to removing our make-up, but they are alarmingly taxing on the environment and most importantly on our waterways. Many people incorrectly dispose of them by flushing them down the toilet, which in turn blocks pipes and causes many fatbergs worldwide. Wet wipes are a large contributor to fatbergs – a congealed mass in a sewer system formed by the combination of non-biodegradable solid matter. So, what's the answer? Ditch the wipes and opt for another more sustainable option when it comes to taking off your make-up. One great alternative is a muslin cloth and a gentle make-up remover.

"Everyday shampoo is not only encased with plastic, but it is also riddled with nasty chemicals like sodium laureth sulfate"

Switch the shampoo

Everyday shampoo is not only encased with plastic, but it is also riddled with nasty chemicals like sodium laureth sulfate (SLS), a common chemical found in many shop-bought shampoos. SLS is popular among many brands as it works as the foaming agent to make your hair soapy, but many of the sulfates are derived from palm oil. Palm oil is incredibly bad for the environment due to the way that it is extracted and the amount of deforestation that occurs in growing the palm. Shampoo also involves using a one-time-use plastic bottle. However, all of this can be avoided by simply switching to shampoo bars, which can be bought as plastic-free products and avoid some of the harmful sulfates.

Sustainable brushing

It may be alarming to read that plastic toothbrushes can take over 400 years to decompose! One of the easiest and simplest steps to make your hygiene routine more eco-friendly is by switching from a plastic brush to a bamboo one. There are so many companies that offer bamboo toothbrushes now, from those with bamboo handles but non-compostable heads that must be cut off, to fully biodegradable brushes. While many of these eco options are yet to hit mainstream supermarket shelves, you can easily find environmentally friendly toothbrushes online or at most health and eco shops on the high street.

MY BATHROOM ROUTINE

Starting today, write down the products that you use as part of your daily routine and then think about plastic free alternatives. Do you use face wipes every day and could replace them with a face cloth and homemade cleanser? Do shampoo bottles litter the shelves in your shower?

Day of the week	What I use now	Plastic-free alternative
Monday		
Tuesday		
wednesday		
Thursday		
friday		
saturday		
sunday		

"Next time you go to wash your hands or brush your teeth, turn the tap off in between"

DRY YOUR TOWELS NATURALLY

Did you know that tumble dryers are one of the most energy-draining appliances in the home? Obviously they are incredibly handy and avoid any washing lurking around on a clothes horse, but it is far more eco-friendly to allow towels to dry naturally. Allowing them to dry naturally also encourages durability of your towels as they take less wear and tear than they would if they went around in a dryer.

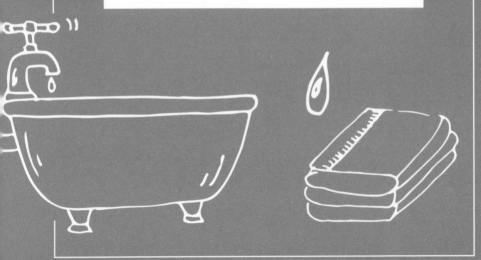

Time your showers

Get yourself an egg timer and set yourself a limit for the amount of time you are spending in your shower every day. Not only will cutting the shower short save you money on your water bill each month, but it will also make a difference to the environment as you will be reducing the amount of energy required to heat the water. This simple switch can be a small step to making your bathroom habits more sustainable as an average shower uses about five gallons of water per minute. Just by shortening your shower to two minutes can cut your water use by ten gallons.

Turn off your tap

Not only can you switch up your routine by opting for more showers over baths to reduce the amount of water you are using, but you can also turn off your tap more elsewhere. Next time you go to wash your hands or brush your teeth, turn the tap off in between.

THAT TIME OF THE MONTH

When you are embarking on a more eco and plastic free lifestyle it's easy to forget about every day items. Women's sanitary products are actually extremely bad for the environment and contribute to a huge amount of plastic pollution. Most women have grown used to using conventional ways of managing their periods such as pads and tampons, however they contain plastic as well as harmful chemicals. Surprisingly pads are actually made of around 90% plastic. Tampons, pads and liners together with their packaging generate more that 200,000 tonnes of waste per year. In recent years many companies have been creating eco-friendly alternatives like reusable pads, reusable tampon applicators, period underwear and menstrual cups. An individual goes through around 11,000 disposable pads or tampons in a lifetime, which equates to a huge amount of waste. Compare this to some menstrual cups that claim to have a 10 year lifetime and the choice is clear.

DIY KITCHEN AND BEAUTY PRODUCTS

A lot of products that we rely on in our daily lives are pumped full of chemicals and nasty ingredients, or come packaged to the brim in plastics and unrecyclable materials. Read on to find out how you can make your own household products to help eliminate plastic waste from your life

Lavender deodorant

Ingredients

- 1 tbsp coconut oil
- 1 tbsp shea butter
- 1 ½ tbsp beeswax
- 5 drops vitamin E oil
- 8 drops lavender Essential oil

1. Place the shea butter, coconut oil and beeswax in a bain marie and heat until melted.

2. Remove from the heat and allow to cool completely.

3. Add the vitamin E oil and the essential oils and mix thoroughly before pouring into a container.

Anti-bacterial spray

Ingredients

- 500ml water
- 1 tbsp witch hazel or white wine vinegar
- 20-30 drops essential oil (tea tree or thyme)

1. Grab yourself an empty plastic spray bottle or reuse an empty one instead.

2. Add witch hazel to the spray bottle, fill with water and swirl to mix.

3. Place 20-30 drops of tea tree oil to the mix and shake well to combine.

4. Give it a test and add more or less essential oils depending on how pungent you want your spray.

Dry shampoo

Ingredients

- 2 tbsp arrowroot/cornstarch
- 2 tbsp cocoa powder
- 5 drops of essential oil of choice (optional – I use lavender)
- An old make-up brush to apply
- Small pot/container to store the dry shampoo

1. **Place the cornstarch with the cocoa powder in a reusable container and give it a mix.**
2. Add the essential oil of your choice to the mix and give it a big shake.
3. **Apply using an old make-up brush, concentrating on the roots that are especially oily.**

Honey sugar scrub

Ingredients

- 2 tbsp honey
- 2 tbsp coconut oil olive oil/sweet almond oil
- 1 cup | 200g brown sugar

1. **Warm the honey slightly in the microwave or over the stove until it becomes slightly runny.**
2. Stir in the sugar and your favourite oil and mix well using a whisk.
3. **Place in the fridge for 20 minutes and once cooled use it on your skin.**

Glass and window cleaner

Ingredients

- 250ml white wine vinegar
- 250ml water

1. **Measure out the white wine vinegar and add to a reusable spray bottle.**
2. Top up the bottle with water and give it a good shake to ensure it has mixed well.
3. **Grab yourself some newspaper or a bit of recycled fabric and put your new DIY spray to the test.**

THE
BIG
CLEAN
UP

When it comes to cleaning our homes, clothes and selves, we've relied on plastic for decades, but now the tide is turning and it's time to go back to the 'old' ways

ne of the reasons many of us are reluctant to adopt a more eco-friendly lifestyle when it comes to cleaning is because it appears less convenient, but it's actually easier than most people realise, and can also benefit your health and bank balance as well as the planet.

Wash away your troubles

One of the most significant threats currently impacting the environment is microplastic, tiny particles shed from plastics in dishwashers and washing machines that eventually find their way into rivers and oceans. Although the effects are not fully known, many scientists predict a raft of long-term health complications. In a bid to reduce the number of microplastics reaching our oceans, there are several things we can do to help.

First, we can stop using plastic plates and cups altogether, or if they are a necessary evil because you have a baby or toddler, rinse them under the tap and reuse them throughout the day , hand-washing where possible. With clothes, try airing them out rather than washing after one wear. When you do use the machine, opt for a cooler temperature and fill the drum to the brim, as less space for clothes to move around in means less chance of fibres breaking off. Likewise forgo using the tumble dryer, which increases fragility.

Containing the problem of containers

As most cleaning fluids are contained within plastic bottles this is where the bulk of the problem lies. Why not buy a reusable spray bottle made of glass, or reuse an existing plastic one and create your own cleaning liquids at home? There are many recipes online, but some of the most effective and relatively inexpensive ones use natural household ingredients. Not only is this better for the environment, but your health too because you won't be touching or inhaling harsh synthetic chemicals.

Top of the swaps

We can all make a difference, big and small, just by implementing a few simple switches to eradicate plastics from our kitchens

WASHING-UP GLOVES
Rubber and latex gloves

Most washing-up gloves that you find in shops contain some form of plastic that cannot be recycled and so usually end up in landfill sites, sometimes after just one wear. True rubber, on the other hand is naturally occuring, biodegradable and renewable because it can be extracted from living trees without causing any damage. As latex is made from rubber, these too are a cost-effective plastic-free alternative the the usual plastic gloves.

PLASTIC BRUSH
Natural material brush

When your plastic washing-up brush gives up the ghost, don't replace it like for like – instead, check out the magnificent bounty of eye-catching and interesting non-plastic options that are out there. For instance, those using a handle made of sustainably sourced wood, metal or ceramic are long-lasting and much better for the planet. What's more, you can find ones with replaceable bristles made of natural fibres such as horse hair or cactus.

MINIMISING MICROPLASTICS

Although there are many microfibre-capturing devices out there (designed to collect the microplastics that come off of your garments in the washing machine), there are conflicting reports as to whether they actually work. As with most things in life, prevention is often better than a cure, so when out shopping for new clothes plump for fabrics made of natural fibres like cotton, wool, silk, linen and hemp, rather than polyester.

YOU LEAVE ME NO CHOICE

If you have to buy plastic-bottled products, look for ones that sport the 'widely recycled' logo, or better yet, choose brands that incentivise customers to return packaging directly to the store, such as cosmetic company The Body Shop, which exchanges five of their empty containers for a £5 voucher. What's more, forgo liquids, particularly household cleaners that bear the warning 'Harmful to aquatic life' – opt for those made with natural ingredients such as Ecover and Method.

WASHING-UP SPONGE
Natural sea sponge

Typically the cheap sponges you find in the supermarket are made from synthetic materials, including plastic that can't be recycled. Instead, spend a little extra and follow the way of our ancestors by using a natural sea sponge. Perfect for scrubbing ourselves, as well plates, these last for a good amount of time, are sustainable, renewable, and biodegradable, so when it's time to renew, just pop your old one on the compost heap.

MICROFIBRE CLOTHS
Cotton cloths

Avoid microfibre cloths and microfibre tea towels like the plague because these are a big contributor to the microplastic crisis, as the plastic particles shed off during the wash and end up in the water supply. Switch out to a cloth that uses sustainably sourced cotton, or even bamboo, instead. Typically these are super soft and fluffy, and can be safely washed in your washing machine or by hand, and therefore can be reused over and over.

LIQUID DETERGENT
Capsules, tablets or powder

Liquid detergent is sold in plastic bottles and often requires the included plastic 'ball' for 'better' results, which increases the production and waste of more plastic. Capsules, however, use a polyvinyl alcohol (PVA) film that breaks down in water. Like a powder detergent, which is added straight to the washer's drawer, the capsule variety are usually sold in cardboard boxes, which can be widely recycled once you've finished a packet.

LIQUID HAND SOAP
Bar of soap

Just as shop-bought cleaning liquids for the home require the use of plastic containers, so do those that we use to clean ourselves. Switching from liquid hand soap to a solid form is a huge step in the right direction. What's more, many ethically focused brands are now producing a growing range of innovative 'naked' (solid) products, including shampoos, conditioners, shower gels, moisturisers and bath bombs.

CLEAN UP
THE NATURAL WAY

Stop buying plastic-bottled household cleaning solutions in store and create your own at home with natural ingredients

KITCHEN DEODORISER

If your sink or fridge has become a little whiffy of late then create your own super simple deodoriser at home. Just mix four tablespoons of baking soda with one litre of warm water. Then pour the solution directly onto the offending surface, give it a good wipe around, then leave to dry.

ALL-PURPOSE HOUSEHOLD CLEANER

Mix one part white vinegar with one part water, lemon rind and a few sprigs of fresh rosemary. Pour into a reusable glass or stainless steel spray bottle, shake and allow to infuse for one week. The fruit acid is perfect for ridding stubborn stains, but is gentle enough to use on most surfaces.

GLASS CLEANER

Mix two cups of water with one cup of white vinegar and for a pleasing scent add a few drops of essential oil, such as orange or lavender. Decant the cleaning solution into a non-plastic spray bottle, target mirrors and windows, and wipe dry with paper towels or even better – a clean cotton cloth.

MOTH REPELLER

Mix one cup of water with several drops of moth-repellent essential oils, such as lavender, lemon and eucalyptus. Soak several small muslin squares in the solution and leave to dry. Later, add fresh lavender, rosemary, mint, thyme, cloves and peppercorns. Secure with string and hang in closets or pop into drawers.

CARPET DEODORISER

This is a fantastic natural fix for pongy carpets, especially great if you have pets. Mix one cup of baking soda with 20 drops of your favourite essential oil (orange and rose are especially nice), and one teaspoon of ground mixed spice. Sprinkle over the carpet, leave for 10 to 15 minutes and vacuum to finish.

GET ORGANISED

Not being organised enough is one of the main reasons why we all fall into the plastic trap. Make a weekly cleaning rota here and write down the plastic free product you'll use.

Day of the week	Cleaning task	Product
Monday		
Tuesday		
Wednesday		
Thursday		
Friday		
Saturday		
Sunday		

GREENER GARDENS

Whether you're a green-fingered guru or a novice, you're likely to come across quite a lot of plastic in the gardening world, but there are so many ways we can do without it

t's fair to say that those who harbour a passion for plants are probably more eager than most to take up the plastic purge challenge. The great news is that there are alternatives for every plastic problem found in the garden.

A plague of pots

The type of plastic most plant pots are made from isn't widely recycled and so the majority end up in landfills. With experts predicting that a plastic plant pot will take up to 450 years to fully biodegrade the outlook is troubling, especially when you consider that 500 million are sold every year. There are biodegradable options, however – some which last a few months and can be planted directly into the soil.

Pest control

Whether it's weeds, insects or birds, there are many pests, which can threaten the potential of your plants, and traditionally plastic has been a key ally in the fight for survival. Netting, weed-control fabric and sprays are some of the most common solutions, but there are natural alternatives to explore. Glass and metal reflective spiralled 'scare' rods that twist and move in the breeze can frighten off birds, or use a wired mesh to protect crops. Suppress weeds with mulch rather than plastic matting, just be sure to opt for the organic version which is composed of formerly living material, such as grass clippings, sawdust and pine needles. The added benefit of mulch is that it delivers a punch of nutrients to the soil as it decomposes, gives bedding an extra layer of warmth in the winter and helps avoid plants drying out in the summer. If you're worried your veg will be munched by an army of insects, consider 'trap' or 'companion' planting before reaching for bottled sprays. By growing sacrificial plants that are easier for the little blighters to feast upon such as nasturtiums and chervil, you stand a better chance of protecting your harvest.

5 TIPS FOR GOING PLASTIC FREE IN YOUR GARDEN

Help your garden really thrive in a completely green and eco-friendly environment

SEEDLING EGG POTS

Eggshells are the perfect replacement for plastic seedling trays. Just add a little compost with the seed, then water, stand it in an old egg box and pop it in your greenhouse or on the windowsill.

WATER BUTTS

Water butts are a wonderful way of collecting rainwater to give to your plants. Not only will this dramatically reduce your water bill, especially in the summer, but many plants actually prefer it to the tap.

LABEL LOVE

Refuse to accept the plastic label when you purchase a plant and make your own instead. Lolly sticks and pegs are simple solutions, or introduce a little creative flair by painting a description or illustration onto a stone or shell.

TOOLS OF THE TRADE

Look for gloves made with leather, rubber or silicone. Plastic-topped tools such as trowels and shears can be replaced for ones with metal or bamboo handles, perhaps featuring a rubber grip for improved comfort and control.

GARDEN FURNITURE AND TOYS

Wooden furniture is seeing a resurgence in popularity thanks to their classical aesthetic. What's more, unlike plastic, wood doesn't fade in the sun, and with a few coats of protective varnishing can go on to survive many decades.

GOING PLASTIC FREE IS CHILD'S PLAY

It's cheap, malleable, strong and versatile so no wonder the vast amount of products aimed at kids are plastic. For those who want better ways to play, however, there are alternatives

ost parents will complain that their children have too much stuff. Christmas and birthdays are responsible for most new additions, but a large volume enter the home sneakily – a freebie attached to a comic, a toy that comes with a meal in a restaurant, a party bag, or possessions passed down from friends and family. Before you know it you're shopping for storage solutions and hide-all furniture to remove the unsightly coloured plastic from view, all the while knowing that most of it won't ever get used. So think of this as a deep cleanse, with the key being: less is more.

Hold back the tide of toys

Sell or donate old plastic toys, and only invest in or accept toys made of non-plastic materials moving forward, such as sustainably sourced wood and plant materials, metal and natural fibres. Unlike novelty and nonsense plastic playthings, those made of other materials tend to focus and sharpen the mind. What's more, they offer a timeless and durable quality plastic can't match, which means they'll last for years.

Painting is a fantastic creative outlet that can be pursued without the need for plastic equipment. Likewise, instead of purchasing modelling clay, make it yourself using water, salt and cornstarch or flour.

Tableware tricks

All children have accidents, and rather than risk injury and the loss of a china plate or glass tumbler, plastic tableware is a cheap and safe substitute. However, plastic poses other problems, namely toxic BPA, microplastics and landfill waste. The good news is that as more consumers adopt a plastic-free outlook, the market has started to shift towards producing innovative alternatives. Organic, sustainably sourced bamboo tableware sets are environmentally friendly, non-toxic and naturally antimicrobial.

3

TOP TIPS FOR GOING PLASTIC FREE WITH THE KIDS

Start them at an early age and make maintaining a plastic-free household the norm for your kids

NAPPIES AND WET WIPES

According to recycling charity Wrap, by the time a child is fully potty trained it's used approximately 6000 disposable diapers, with an estimated four billion nappies thrown away in the UK every year, which end up in landfills or are burnt. If you're dedicated to forge ahead with a plastic-free lifestyle then the answer is biodegradable or cloth nappies, such as 100% cotton terry cloth, which can be washed (on a full load in an energy efficient machine) and reused. What's more, like wet, surface and face wipes, baby wipes contain plastic and take over 100 years to biodegrade in landfill or cause blockages and pollution when flushed down a toilet, so campaigners are calling for a complete ban. The more environmentally friendly solution is to use reusable cloths or wipes sporting the 'fine to flush' logo.

KIDS AGAINST PLASTIC

Our children are the future, and how we guide and educate them today can have a huge impact on all of our tomorrows, so it's never been more important to get children excited about saving the environment. Point them towards children-led action groups like 'Kids Against Plastic', which aims to empower young people in inspiring all of us to be 'plastic clever'.

REWARDS FOR RECYCLING

For kids that need motivating why not start a reward chart? There are free print outs online or try creating your own. For example, draw out a rectangle on a piece of recycled paper and dissect it with a series of horizontal and vertical lines to make several dozen squares. In each square draw or write a reward, such as 'three bedtime stories', 'baking with Mummy' or 'board game with Daddy'. Every time they recycle something or do something beneficial for the environment like turn off a light or ask to walk somewhere instead of the car, they get to place a biodegradable sticker or use a rubber stamp to mark their accomplishment on their chart and gain a reward.

PETS
WITHOUT
THE
PLASTIC

Pets bring so much joy to our lives but also a lot of accessories, so here's some advice for how to make sure none of it is plastic based

t's estimated there are over 51 million pets living in the UK, so it's no wonder that the pet industry is big business, with experts predicting that by 2023 pet products and services sold in the UK will surpass the £2 billion mark. From toys to poop bags, food packaging to cleaning solutions, plastic features heavily in almost all products pitched at pets, which is becoming a growing concern as many items still can't be widely recycled. But there are plastic-free alternatives that are sure to keep any pet pleased.

Toys, cages and bowls, oh my!

Most pet toys are likely to be made chiefly of plastic, sold in plastic packaging and with plastic tags. But there are alternatives. Look for gifts made of rubber or silicone. In the case of cages, toys or items that need to be tougher, like food bowls, plump for metals and woods (such as bamboo), or you could even give rice husk a try, which may not be as tough, but is biodegradable. Many pet beds contain hidden plastics, so a far better option is to create one yourself, using items such as an old leather suitcase, a wooden crate or a cut-in-half old oak wine barrel for the frame. Fill with pillows and blankets for a snuggly interior.

Food for thought

The bulk of pet food and pet treats are sold in plastic packaging; be it dried food or single-serving 'wet' food pouches, which according to a report by The Times, fewer than 1 in 20,000 are recycled, despite many of the plastic packets claiming to be made of recyclable material. One of the most obvious and easily accessed alternatives is food sold in aluminium cans, or if you travel to a specific pet food store you should find large tubs of dry food that you can decant into a reusable container and pay by the kilo. Alternatively you could cook you pet's food. This is especially beneficial if your pet has a health condition. Head online to find a plethora of recipes perfect for your pet. Bon apawtit!

5 TOP TIPS FOR GOING PLASTIC-FREE WITH YOUR PETS

Follow our simple advice for avoiding plastic products with your furry friends

HAMSTER BALLS

When it comes to hamster balls, you aren't likely to find a plastic-free alternative to the spherical, perspex containers. A better option is to build an enclosed area for the hamster to run about freely.

SHAMPOO, RINSE AND REPEAT

When it comes to cleaning your animal, keep it old school with a bar of soap, but look for specific pet shampoo bars, which are milder than our own, and feature a bounty of natural ingredients.

LEAD ASTRAY

Animal leads are primarily made of nylon. A plastic-free alternative would be a metal-clasped leash made of natural-fibre rope or hemp, which are both machine washable, and the latter is thought to be anti-bacterial.

POOP IT ON THE COMPOST HEAP

Although dog and cat poop shouldn't be chucked on the compost pile, you can add poop from rabbits, hamsters, gerbils and guinea pigs, as long as they have been fed a vegetarian diet.

Pet Food

DIY PET FOOD

Cater for your pet's tastes by creating bespoke meals at home. Look online for suggestions or purchase a specific cookbook. Make sure you know what your pet's diet should include and more importantly, what it shouldn't include.

PLASTIC-
FREE LIFESTYLE

Opting for plastic is
often the easy option,
but let's explore how
you can change this

TIME TO PART-Y WITH PLASTIC

A big occasion like a birthday or a wedding can be a minefield when it comes to plastic. Read on to find out some handy tips to host a plastic-free party

hatever your age, a birthday party is guaranteed to contain plastic, from plates and cutlery to balloons and banners. But don't worry, as there's lots you can do to reduce the amount of plastic used. Start by using crockery and glassware instead of single-use plastic alternatives – you'll just have to deal with the washing up afterwards! If you don't have enough glasses to cater for all your friends, most good supermarkets now run glassware hire schemes, with some shops even offering it for free.

Meanwhile Majestic Wine offers a free hire and delivery service as long as you order your booze with them. If that wasn't enough, the company also offers a 'Sale and Return' service on anything unopened at the end of your party.

As for children's birthday parties, make sure your party bags are paper ones instead of plastic and try and include plastic-free gifts or sweets in recyclable packaging. Don't forget to swap plastic straws for metal, paper, wheat or bamboo alternatives.

Weddings

In October 2018, Princess Eugenie and husband Jack Brooksbank held a plastic-free wedding, but it isn't just the royal family who can achieve such a feat. You can start with the hen do, making sure that you ditch the plastic memorabilia for paper and wooden alternatives. For example, photo props are fun but can be made without plastic. Suggestive straws however, cannot, but you can have just as good a time without them!

Then there's the wedding outfits, which can contain a surprisingly significant amount of hidden plastic thanks to synthetic fibres such as polyester. Try to choose a dress made from natural and organic materials, such as silk, and avoid any embellishments that are made from plastic, such as sequins where possible. Adopt the same approach when it comes to your bridesmaids, groom and groomsmen's outfits.

"Cocktail sticks made from wood or bamboo are perfect for replacing plastic cutlery when it comes to finger food"

As for the wedding venue, make sure you check what the recycling policy is for the premises, so you know as much as possible will be done with the inevitable waste. When it comes to decorating your venue, avoid balloons and other plastic accessories and opt for more eco-friendly decorations, such as empty glass jars filled with tealights, eco-friendly confetti – which can easily be bought online – and fairy lights.

With flowers, if you are doing your own arrangements you should head to a local flower market or florist and bulk-buy ones without cellophane wrapping. Another alternative would be filling your venue with potted plants and herbs, which could then be given as gifts to your guests at the end of the day.

Christmas

Christmas may only be one day but it produces a heck of a lot of plastic, from the packaging our food comes in to how we wrap our presents – not to mention Christmas tree decorations! For the latter, go for a more natural look with sprigs of holly and fir, twigs and branches, mistletoe and pine cones, rather than plastic baubles. As for the tree itself, if you have an artificial one, get as many years out of it as possible, and if you buy a real one, make sure it's got an FSC logo or one approved by the Soil Association.

Present-wise, try giving loved ones gift experiences rather than items that need wrapping. Saying that, buying items that could encourage your family and friends to reduce their plastic usage all-year-round would be a winning idea; think about funky reusable water bottles and coffee cups, tote bags and beauty products made by brands that use recycled plastic.

If you do have to wrap things up, go old school with brown paper and twine or ribbon cloth. You can also recycle old Christmas cards to use as gift tags.

As for your festive food, buy vegetables loose to avoid unnecessary plastic packaging. If you're throwing a party, opt for canapés and finger foods over things in plastic tubs and containers like dips and pre-packed sausage rolls. You could also do a cheeseboard with homemade crackers, chutneys and grapes. Cocktail sticks made from wood or bamboo are perfect for replacing plastic cutlery when it comes to finger food.

Other easy-to-make nibbles instead of buying packaged supermarket versions include truffles, mince pies, crudités, sweet potato wedges and bruschetta.

SPARKLE THE RIGHT WAY

What would a party be without glitter? Sadly environmentalists say glitter is a microplastic making its way into our seas and affecting marine life. Microplastics are fragments of plastic less than 5mm in length and can easily be swallowed by marine life, proving fatal to them. It could potentially enter the food chain too. Thankfully a number of brands now sell eco-friendly glitter, including Eco Glitter Fun and EcoStardust Biodegradable Glitter. Both sell a wide range of colours and blends as well as using recyclable packaging and donating a portion of their proceeds to environmental projects.

AVOID HALLOWEEN HORRORS

Halloween is hellish for plastic. Shop-bought costumes are made of synthetic fibres, so try making your own with old fabrics. Avoid artificial pumpkins and buy real ones instead – carving them can be a fun family activity! For trick or treat, swap packaged sweets for Halloween-themed homemade biscuits.

10

TIPS TO BE A PLASTIC-FREE PARTY PLANNING BOSS

CHOOSE THE RIGHT TIPPLE

Go plastic-free with refillable jugs of water and glass-bottled soft drinks. As for alcohol, make sure your wine bottles are corked not screw tops, and buy lager and beer in boxes, not in plastic rings.

GET RID OF PLASTIC GARMENT BAGS

Wedding gowns, suits and bridesmaid dresses regularly come in plastic bags, which will immediately be chucked away. To be more environmentally friendly, buy reusable clothing and suit bags instead.

DITCH THE DISPOSABLE BBQS

Barbecuing is a favourite British summer pastime, but to be as plastic-free as possible, don't buy disposable barbecues. Instead, buy one made from wood, which can be used as a campfire afterwards.

SWAP YOUR STRAWS

Plastic straws are one of the easiest things to banish. As well as metal straws, The Wheat Straws Company sells compostable, biodegradable, natural and gluten-free wheat straws, which stay solid for hours.

PLASTIC-FREE PICNIC ESSENTIALS

Picnics are rife with single-use plastic, but you can replace them in many ways. Food wraps are a great alternative to cling film, while plastic containers can be switched out for stainless steel ones from places like Elephant Box.

> "You can buy biodegradable confetti, which is safer for the environment and wildlife"

GO PREPARED ON YOUR FOOD SHOP

Whatever occasion you are buying food for, packaging is hard to avoid. Take your own containers to butchers, bakers or supermarket fresh food counters and ask them to use those instead.

BE A CONFETTI QUEEN

Get creative and create your own confetti to be thrown outside the wedding venue. All you need to do is get some dried flowers, old book pages and a hole punch. If that's too fiddly a task, you can buy biodegradable confetti, which is safer for the environment and wildlife.

WRAP IT RIGHT

To decorate your own wrapping paper, make your own designs with a potato print on eco-friendly paper. Alternatively, wrap a present in paper relevant to the recipient, like an old copy of *Vogue* or an old comic book.

HAVE A CRACK AT MAKING YOUR OWN

Christmas crackers are another festive item full of plastic, but they don't have to be bad. Not only can you get ones made from recycled materials, you can also make your own! There are several kits to choose from online.

BIG CHANGES FOR YOUR BIG DAY

As well as choosing wedding outfits made of sustainable fabrics, you can reduce plastic when it comes to toiletries and cosmetics. Opt for brands which use recycled plastic or plastic-free packaging.

GET PARTY PLANNING

Use this space to make a plastic-free party plan

Occassion	Theme	Date	Location	Number of guests

SHOPPING LIST

PARTY ITINERARY

PLASTIC-FREE TRAVEL AND CAMPING

Whether you're on your holidays, camping with family or hitting the festivals, being away from home doesn't mean you have to resort to using plastic products

lastic-free or reduced-plastic travel has never been easier. It just takes a little pre-planning and organisation. There are so many simple ideas that you can use whether you are going out for the day or travelling for a month.

Toiletries, for example, can be overhauled fairly simply. Don't buy into 'travel size' products. Instead, make your own eco-friendly toiletry kit you can take with you wherever you go. A bamboo toothbrush in its own case is a great start. Shampoo bars and soap in their own individual tins take up less room in your suitcase than conventional bottles. If you do use products that need a bottle, invest in a set of reusable ones and fill with what you need.

Eco camping

If you're going camping, there are so many ways you can start to ditch the plastic. It's easy to fall into the trap of buying camping-specific items, but often there is no need. You can pack your usual cups, cutlery, cloth napkins and reusable bottles, rather than buying anything new. Saying that, you may wish to invest in a good outdoor bamboo dining set if you don't want to risk breaking your best plates.

If you can, prepare foods before you go and store in your own sustainable packaging. See our boxout for some top meals to prepare in advance. As well as these meal ideas, you can stock up on the basics, which for camping should include oats, pasta, rice and eggs (which you can get from dedicated package-free shops). All of these you can take in your own containers and they provide filling, easy-to-cook options for all times of the day. Consider taking some beeswax wraps with you so you can wrap any food you need to, in place of alternatives like cling film. Get hold of a good, large water container, so you can make a trip to the camp drinking water tap, fill it up and have it on hand to cook with and refill water bottles as you need to.

Cleaner festivals

Festivals mean packing light, but it doesn't mean you have to be plastic heavy. When it comes to food, you probably won't be cracking out the camping stove. If you're eating on site, consider carrying your own cutlery so you're not reliant on disposable options. Take a refillable water bottle, a reusable coffee cup and pack a few snacks in your own small containers.

Pack a small cloth bag you can use for dirty clothing. It might also be useful to have another cloth bag in case you end up buying anything extra. And don't even think about bin bags or plastic ponchos for rain cover – be prepared and invest in a decent packaway coat that you can stash in your main bag.

Washing on a festival site can be difficult, with limited access to showers. Take a flannel you can wet for a quick wash, rather than wet wipes. You can also get microfibre towels, which pack down very small but open out to a decent size.

One of the biggest problems after a festival is the number of tents left behind. If your tent breaks, see if there is a dedicated recycling point at your festival – many will collect them to be disposed of responsibly or given to charity. Ideally, however, you should take home everything you bring with you. Most tents that are broken can be fixed and this will mean you have a functional tent for your next festival.

Day tripping

Even if you're just heading out for a day with the family, make sure you have everything you need on you to reduce your plastic use. Packing a picnic is a great first step, as you will be able to prepare your own food in your own containers, saving on buying plastic-wrapped foods when out and about.

If you're heading to the beach, don't forget the suncream. You can now get products that are in biodegradeable packaging, so you don't have to reply on plastic-packed supermarket specials. Also, make sure that you pack some toys for the kids to play with – the 99p bucket and spade sets from the beach shop will break and end up in landfill far too quickly.

Combined with the other tips over these pages, we're sure you'll soon find plastic-free travel becomes second nature.

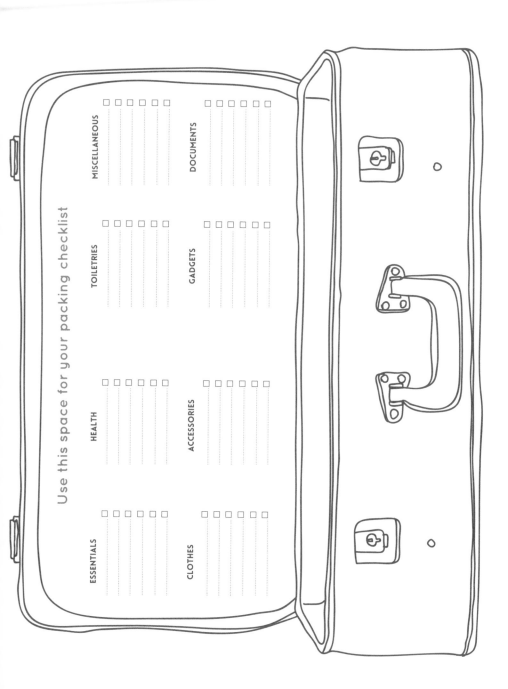

Use this space for your packing checklist

ESSENTIALS

HEALTH

TOILETRIES

MISCELLANEOUS

CLOTHES

ACCESSORIES

GADGETS

DOCUMENTS

5

WAYS TO REDUCE YOUR USE OF PLASTIC ON A TRIP

The key to eco-friendly travel is being prepared before you set off

A plastic-free lifestyle is not without its challenges. Going out and about, especially when travelling away from home, can definitely present a few obstacles. The trick is to anticipate all the potential situations you might face and have a plan on how to deal with them. This mostly comes down to becoming a pro at eco-friendly packing. Whether you're on a day trip or week-long overseas jaunt, you can reduce the plastic you need to take with you and use when you're there with these top tips.

CARRY YOUR OWN BOTTLE

Invest in a good reusable bottle that you can take with you wherever you go. Don't be afraid to ask in bars, restaurants and cafes for a refill if there are no public fountains available. If you are advised not to drink the tap water, use a kettle to boil the water to purify it.

PACK AN EXTRA BAG

Simple cloth bags take up no room at all, so make sure that you always have one to hand. You never know when you will need an extra bag for a spot of unexpected shopping or to pack lunch in.

BUY A PORTABLE CUTLERY SET

You can get small, compact cutlery sets that slip in your bag. They usually come in their own case to stop the parts getting lost. Look for the stainless steel or bamboo versions, rather than plastic.

GET A SET OF CLOTH HANDKERCHIEFS

The old-fashioned handkerchief is back in favour. Carry a couple in your bag at all times to use as a tissue, in place of wet wipes, to clean spills and so much more. They can be easily washed and reused, and they take up little space in your bag.

TAKE A REUSABLE COFFEE CUP

Like the water bottle above, invest in a decent coffee cup. Most takeaway coffee shops will let you use your own container, and often offer a discount for doing so. You can get collapsible ones, so they fold down to save space in your bag.

JUST SAY NO

Hotels and flights are often rife with single-use plastic, from disposable cutlery to the free shampoo and in-room bottles of water. You can very simply start to reduce your plastic use by opting not to use these items and rely on your own personal plastic-free alternatives instead.

5 PLASTIC-FREE-FRIENDLY TRAVEL DESTINATIONS

We round up the top countries that are actively setting targets to reduce plastic waste across their lands and waters

Aiming to reduce the use of single-use plastics is high on the agenda of most major countries, but some are taking larger steps than others. Travelling to far-flung destinations means making journeys that produce harmful emissions, so we have the responsibility to ensure we're doing our best to offset our travels. One way that we can do this is by ensuring that we tread lightly in our chosen destinations, leaving no footprint and no waste. Being aware of which countries have plastic-free policies can be useful, as you know you will be able to avoid using single-use plastic while travelling more easily. We have highlighted just five countries that have hit the headlines thanks to their advances in the battle against single-use plastics – no one country is perfect, but we're heartened to see the strides being made, especially by those that had previously been among the worst offenders in the battle against plastic.

COSTA RICA

One of the most eco-driven, sustainable destinations in the world, Costa Rica launched a national strategy, led by its government, to be single-use-plastic free by 2021. This is alongside its initiatives that are increasing forest coverage and reducing carbon emissions. It was announced as the UN's Champion of the Earth in 2019 for Policy Leadership.

CANADA

The country-wide Strategy on Zero Plastic Waste was approved at the end of 2018, with ambitious plans to reduce single-use plastic waste in Canada. The impact of this is already being seen across the country, turning its previously undesirable eco credentials right around. The focus is on recycling, recovering and reusing plastic, as well as exploring alternatives.

KENYA

Kenya hit the headlines for its hard-line approach to banning plastic bags – with large fines and even prison sentences for selling, manufacturing or carrying single-use bags. The impact has been huge, clearing streets and waterways, and even preventing the consumption of bags by livestock.

FRANCE

Leading the way in Europe, France has banned all single-use plastic cups, cutlery and plates from 2020, the first country in the world to do so. It also has penalties on goods and produce wrapped in non-recycled plastic, with recycled-packaged products cheaper to buy, so is an ideal plastic-free destination.

SWEDEN

Sweden aims to become a completely waste-free society, and its recycling programs are the best in the world. 47% of all its plastic is recycled (compared to, for example, 25% in France). This is helped by projects such as can and bottle deposit schemes and 'circular economy' systems.

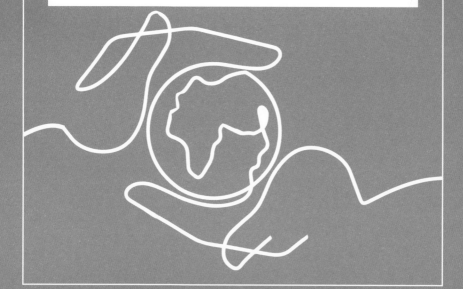

RESPONSIBLE RECYCLING

Learn what to do with your plastic waste and get upcycling with our simple projects

HOW TO RECYCLE RESPONSIBLY

Our homes are full of plastic these days, and while it's unrealistic to be completely plastic-free, there's lots you can do to reduce your intake and help the environment

nderstanding the different types of plastic can be difficult, as your bottle of water is made from a different plastic to your margarine tub. Items have triangle symbols made up of arrows printed on them, and the number in the centre as well as the letters underneath reveal what kind of plastic it is, and how easy it is to recycle.

For example, plastic bottles including pop and mouthwash – as well as some yoghurt tubs – are 1-PET, the easiest to recycle, while 2-HDPE applies to items like shampoo bottles, milk jugs and margarine tubs. While they are recyclable, you need to check they can be processed in your area with your local authority.

How to recycle at home

It simply isn't enough to just dump all your plastic in a recycling bin and see that as doing your bit. If a plastic container is covered in too much residue, it could stop it being recycled, so make sure that you are giving any plastic bottles, tubs or containers a thorough rinse out with water before putting them in the recycling bin.

E-WASTE

"Retailers and brands are obliged to provide customers with an option of recycling their old electronics"

It's a good idea to squash down any plastic bottles so they don't fall off the sorting conveyor belts at the recycling plants, too. You should also push any plastic straws down into its carton, and screw plastic bottle tops back on before chucking the bottles away as this can help with the sorting process.

Once at a recycling centre, plastics are sorted into polymer types, then shredded, washed, melted and pelletised. In this new state, they are then ready to be turned into new products.

You don't have to throw all your plastic away though! Plastic takeaway containers can be reused for lunches and leftovers, while empty water bottles can be repurposed and upcycled – read on to discover several fun projects to give plastic bottles a new lease of life.

How to recycle electronic goods

Our homes are full of other items which contain plastic, such as mobile phones, games consoles, TVs and laptops. These can also be recycled, with responsible recycling of waste electrical and electronic equipment – or WEEE for short – now a major environmental goal. By recycling your WEEE properly instead of just putting it in your rubbish bin, you will help stop our land, water and air becoming contaminated.

You can recycle anything from small gadgets, such as DVD players and remote controls, to large appliances, such as fridges, freezers and washing machines. Smaller appliances like kettles, toasters, hairdryers and straighteners can also be recycled, but if you're unsure, take it to your local recycling centre and ask a staff member. As a general rule, anything with a plug or requiring batteries for power can be recycled.

Many residential flat complexes have special bins for smaller appliances, while larger items can either be taken to your local recycling centre or a specialist waste disposal company can arrange to come and collect them.

Since 2003, retailers and brands are obliged to provide customers with an option of recycling their old electronics when purchasing a new one. Many offer a collection service or drop off facility in store.

Recycling clothing

In the UK, 235 million items of clothing were sent to landfill in Spring 2017, meaning it's more important than ever to recycle your clothing and unwanted textiles.

The first port of call can be charity shops or collection bags, as charities are able to sort out what can be resold. Anything that can't is sold to textile recycling companies. Some councils also offer clothing collection services as part of their recycling programme.

However, more and more garments are made with polyester, which isn't a sustainable textile option because it is made with PET, the most common type of plastic, and the more synthetic fabrics it's blended with, the harder it is to recycle. If you can reduce the amount of synthetic fabrics you buy in the first place, that will help the environment. If you do buy garments made from such fabrics, make sure you recycle them as best you can to avoid landfill.

The other alternative is upcycling your clothes, which means mending or altering a garment to make it wearable again rather than chucking it away.

WHERE CAN I RECYCLE?

Make a note of where you can recycle locally

Recycling location	Item

EIGHT FANTASTIC UPCYCLING PROJECTS

It's always important to recycle any plastic you have, but why not go one step further? Try these home projects to upcycle common plastic waste into something cool

The average person uses 100 kilograms of pure plastic per year, and most of it won't be recycled. The time that a single-use plastic item (such as a bottle of water or soft drink) is used by the consumer (as little as five minutes) is a tiny fraction of the centuries that the same bottle will take to decompose as rubbish. While most people are aware of the need to recycle, and will be making better efforts to do so, another use for your old plastic is to upcycle it. Rather than returning them to be reduced into their components, upcycling helps you find a whole new life for your old plastic products, one that is much longer lasting than the single use it was designed for.

Upcycling is a wonderful way to think about our world and our collective impact on it. It is the principle of taking an item that you no longer need, and turning it into something else, ideally something that will last for months or even years. The projects below are all manageable and don't require huge resources (other than patience, time, and some household supplies). They will also help you think about the principle of upcycling, and inspire you to find innovative new uses for your old things.

HANGING PLANTERS

Build your own herb garden, or brighten up your balcony using plastic bottles

This is an excellent way to advertise your sustainable lifestyle, inspire others, and produce you own home-grown herbs for cooking. With a few artistic labels, you will be ready to show off your own living spice rack. Alternatively, you can add some colour to your balcony or patio with some easy-growing flowers. These are very easy to make, don't take a lot of materials, and you can just add more columns whenever you feel like it.

YOU WILL NEED:

Lots of
plastic bottles
(no smaller
than 1.5-2l)

Garden wire

Wire cutters

Potting soil seeds
(depending on the
type of hanging
garden you want to
make, e.g., herbs,
flowers)

Nails

Stanley/kitchen knife

Scissors

Marker pen

Paper

Decide where you're going to hang your garden

This can be almost anywhere, although it's a good idea to hang your columns either outdoors or over a non-carpeted area (such as by a kitchen window).

Sort your bottles

Decide how many planters you want in each column. If you have different shaped bottles, decide how you want to arrange them, perhaps using a grid on a piece of paper, and consider how much vertical space you want between each planter (determined by how much wire you use in Step 5).

Make your stencil

Draw an opening on one side of a bottle. Put your first bottle on its side. The side facing upwards is the top of the planter, which is where your opening will be. When this is cut, it will open up a large part of the bottle. Draw it to your design, make a copy of the outline by tracing it onto a piece of paper. Cut the paper so your outline is all that's left.

Draw & cut your outlines

Draw around your stencil on each of your bottles in the same spot on each bottle. When they all look the same, cut the openings out using the Stanley/kitchen knife and scissors. You should now have a collection of bottle planters – now you need to attach them!

Make four holes

Using a nail, poke four holes in each planter. The positions of the holes should be on either side of the opening.

Prepare your wires

How much space you leave between each planter will be up to you, but make sure that you have enough wire to make a large knot at either end. Whichever knot you decide to use (a double should be strong enough), make sure that all the lengths of wire are the same.

Make your planters hang

You'll need two lengths of wire per planter. Push the wire through the hole made by the nail on the top of the planter. Tie a double knot and do the same on the other side. You should now have a planter hanging from two wires, the opening facing upwards. Repeat for all planters.

Hang them in a column

Using the same knot, tie your planter to the bottom holes of the planter above it. Repeat for all planters until you have your hanging column. Now you can hang your column where you decided in Step 1. If you need anchor points, make them with nails, using your hammer.

Add potting soil and seeds

Your potting soil should fill the bottom half of the planter, then add the seeds and a bit of water. Now you just need to wait!

ORGANISERS

Milk containers and plastic bottles can be easily turned into stylish organisers

We use so many plastic bottles and cartons in our homes without ever considering what we can do with them once we've finished. Any coloured plastic can easily be turned into a useful container, and each is an opportunity to let you express your creativity. By upcycling these items into organisers, you have the chance to make personalised additions to every room of the home.

YOU WILL NEED:

A variety of milk bottle cartons or plastic bottles

Knife

Scissors

Steam iron

Optional: Craft paper and glue gun

Cut to your desired size

Using a knife, cut the top portion from your bottle. The tallest point of your organiser should be approximately one inch below the smallest object you plan to keep in it.

Use steam iron to create new rim

Use the steam iron on high heat. Place the newly cut rim of your organiser on the iron for three to five seconds maximum. This will create a smooth and rounded edge.

Decorate

This can be in any way you like. If you want to disguise the origins of your organiser using craft paper, use a strong adhesive. If the bottle used is made of see-through plastic, then consider minimum decoration, so you can see all of the objects inside the organiser.

BOTTLE BIRD FEEDER

Liven up your garden or balcony space with this simple bird feeder made from an old bottle

Most birds love a birdfeeder, and they're an attractive addition to any garden. This one is very simple to make, and when you see how easy it is, you'll be looking for even more branch space!

YOU WILL NEED:

Plastic bottle

String

Scissors

Birdseed

2 or 3 wooden spoons

1. Create holes and perch

For each spoon, create two holes on opposite sides of the bottle. This can be done by piercing the bottle with the scissors and inserting the spoon through, which will make the structure secure. Make a slightly larger hole for the bowl (wider end) and have it facing up so it can contain a bit of birdseed.

2. Add birdseed

Fill the bottle with birdseed. A few grains of birdseed should sit naturally in the bowl of the spoon if the larger hole is made.

3. Create a handle and hang

There are a couple of ways to do this. You can either make a tight knot around the rim of the bottle, or cut a couple of holes near the top of the bottle and run the string through. Tie this in a loop then you are ready to hang it on your favourite tree. Birds will likely appear within a few days of you hanging it up.

As most plastic drinks bottles should not be used again for storing water, this is a much better and safer use for them.

STYLISH STENCIL LAMPS

You'll be surprised how easy these professional-looking lamps are to make

These lamps should be on everybody's project list. They are so simple to make, and yet are so unique and effective. You aren't limited to white light, either. Although these lamps look fantastic in white, there is no reason you can't experiment with other colours using translucent tissue paper as your lower (second) layer. This lamp can therefore fit in any room of your home, and make brilliant personalised gifts for friends and family.

YOU WILL NEED:

Two-litre plastic bottle with labels removed

Thin card/craft paper (two per lamp)

Scissors

Stencil designs

Christmas/fairy lights (must have LED bulbs)

Glue

1 Remove bottle top

Cut off the top of the bottle to make a cylinder. If using mains-powered lights, make a hole at the base of the bottle also, to allow the plug to go through.

2 Place lights inside

Arrange the lights in a way you find appealing.

3 Prepare layers

Wrap your plastic cylinder with one layer of card/paper and mark the size you need, allowing the paper to extend 1.5 inches beyond the top of the top of the cylinder, and reach to the bottom. Cut two pieces of paper/thin card to these measurements.

Create stencil layer

Using your stencil and pencil, be as creative as you like to make a pattern or design. One attractive option is several hexagons arranged in a partial-honeycomb design.

Cut stencil layer

Using the Stanley knife, carefully cut out the shapes in your stencil layer. Take your time, and make sure you do this on a surface that is both clean and can be marked.

Glue layers

Using glue around all edges of the stencil layer, place this on top of the second layer. Leave to dry.

Wrap layers around cylinder

Apply glue around the top rim of the cylinder and at the bottom of the cylinder. Wrap it with the layers and hold in place until dry.

"This lamp can therefore fit in any room of your home, and make brilliant personalised gifts for friends and family"

PLASTIC BAG ROPE

Whatever you use rope or wool for, this is an
excellent way to turn plastic bags into yarn

With knitting and crochet becoming a more common hobby, it's never too soon to start learning for yourself. You'll also be helping the planet by upcycling the plastic bags that are no longer needed.

YOU WILL NEED:

Multiple single-use
plastic bags

Scissors

1. Prepare your bags

Cut off the handles and the fused bottom of the bag. This will make a tube shape of plastic. Cut the rest of the bag into smaller hoops of 3-5cm width. Do this for all of the bags you want to upcycle.

2. Begin twisting

Take the first circular hoop and hold it in both hands at opposite ends, pinching the width in the middle. Twist the plastic in opposite directions. Continue to twist until the middle of the plastic begins to bunch up and twist.

3. Connect to the next strand

Once you've gotten to end of your plastic you should have two small loops in your hands. Feed the larger one through the smaller one and pull slightly to create a larks head knot. Then use the same method to connect the last loop to the centre of the next plastic circle.

4. Continue twisting

Use the same method of twisting on the new strand of plastic. The end of the new strand made from twisting should form around where the last strand met. Continue to do this until you run out of bags. Use your new rope for whatever you like!

Wrap the plastic rope around plant pots to give them a refresh or use it to tether the ultimate blanket fort for your kids

PIGGY-BOTTLE BANK
Craft your own piggy bank and save for that
next guilty purchase!

YOU WILL NEED:

Plastic bottle
with cap

4 bottle caps

Cardboard

Pink paint & brush/
pink spray cannister

Glue

Sticky tape

Black marker pen

Stanley knife

The most fun way to save any loose change or small
notes is using a piggy bank. What could be better
than one you can make yourself?

Prepare bottle

Take off any labels. Make sure that the
largest sized coin you plan to put in the
piggy bank will fit through the bottleneck.
Circular juice bottles can be good for this.

Add the feet

Stick four bottle caps to the bottom of the
bottle. Alternatively, make short legs out of
strips cardboard with four small holes, using
the scissors and then poke the legs through.

Make a coin slot

On the top of the
"back" (opposite
side of bottle from
the feet) cut a slot
using the Stanley/
kitchen knife.

Ears and tail

Make these by
cutting two
triangles and a
small spiral out
of the cardboard.
The ears are made
by folding one of
the sides up and
gluing them to the
base of the bottle
neck towards the
coin slot. The tail is
glued to the centre
of the base.

Decorate!

Paint the entire
pig. When dry,
add trotters,
eyes and nostrils
simply using the
black marker pen.

Encourage your
kids to think
up creative
upcycling ideas

OTTOMAN

If you're feeling ambitious, make some furniture for your living space or bedroom

If you're a novice sewist, or want to take up the craft, this is the perfect way to hone those skills, as learning the skills needed for measurement and sewing will be a by-product of this project.

YOU WILL NEED:

Plastic bottles
(2-litre bottles)

Foam sheets

Cardboard

Wide sticky tape

Sewing gear
Sewing gear (either
needle & thread, or a
machine)

Your own choice
of fabrics (one
underlayer, one
top layer)

1. Create the centre

Arrange the bottles in a pattern where they are all touching as many other bottles as possible with the tops facing up. Use sticky tape to bind them all in together.

2. Add a cardboard base and top

Using big pieces of cardboard, make a circle for the top and bottom of your ottoman. Secure them to the ottoman using sticky tape.

3. Cover in foam

Using the sticky tape and foam sheets, make a nice comfortable cushion and sides for your ottoman.

4. Sew your fabric underlayer

Measure out the fabric you will need for the underlayer, and sew it around the ottoman centre.

5. Design and sew your top layer

Pick fabrics that match your living or bedroom to decorate, or a bright colour!

Turn bottle tops into fridge magnets or why not make a simple game of ticltackltoe using 10 bottle tops and magnet

YOGURT POT? HERB POT!

Always attractive on a kitchen window and very easy to upcycle, this pot is a must-make

Whatever the herb, or even spice that you want to grow, this pot is so easy to craft you might run out of herbs that you want to pot!

YOU WILL NEED:

Large yogurt pot (500g)

Scissors

Steam iron

Coarse string

Small paint brush

Potting soil

Herb/succulent

Optional:
Glue gun, metal ribbon

1. Clean the yogurt pot

The best way to do this is to eat the contents, followed by a thorough wash.

2. Cut to the desired size

Take off the top third of the yogurt pot using the scissors. Use the steam iron on a high heat for three to five seconds to create a new rim to your pot, as with Project 2.

3. Prepare your glue palette

Use the old yogurt top as a palette for your glue. Pour glue on the top and prepare your brush.

4. Pot decoration

Add glue and wind the coarse string tightly from the top rim downwards. Repeat until the pot is complete.

5. Add soil and herbs

Fill the potting soil to half an inch below the rim, and plant the seeds. Why not try growing some chillies?

With a small amount of sewing, an old t-shirt can easily become a fashionable reusable bag

BE INSPIRED
Find out more about
the campaigners
and companies leading
the way to change

Discover how everyone from campaigners and small businesses to global industries are tackling the impact of single-use plastic on the world we share

t is no secret that the lifestyle that we enjoy generates a lot of waste, and the pressure is building for all of us to live in a more sustainable way. One of the biggest impacts on the environment is plastic. Unlike natural materials, plastic is a human-made component that is incredibly durable, and takes hundreds of years to decompose naturally. Plastic is therefore one of the most destructive influences upon the environment. Of the billions of metric tons of plastic that has been produced, only 9% of it is recycled. However, there are entrepreneurs, campaigners, small businesses and global corporations who are all working to address this issue before the damage to the environment is irreparable.

12
COMPANIES AND CAMPAINGERS THAT ARE LEADING THE PLASTIC FIGHT

BOYAN SLAT
The Ocean Cleanup

Boyan Slat is the mind behind The Ocean Cleanup project. He has been building machines for a long time, and dropped out of his engineering degree in order to focus on The Ocean Cleanup. This project centres around autonomous floating barriers that combine various technologies with ocean currents in order to "catch" floating plastic in the sea. The barriers are entirely solar-powered and use algorithms based on wind and sea current to hone in on masses of floating plastic. Slat is the CEO of The Ocean Cleanup, which initially raised $2 million through crowdfunding to support the idea when his TEDx talk went viral. This was boosted to over $31 million by donations from other entrepreneurs and technology companies. Aged just 25, Slat's company has recently launched the second large-scale prototype barrier with promising results.

ELLEN MACARTHUR
New Plastics Economy Global Commitment

Dame Ellen MacArthur is a celebrated yachtsman who broke the world record for fastest solo circumnavigation of the Earth in 2005. She retired from sailing in 2010 and established the Ellen MacArthur Foundation, which focuses on establishing circular economies (where the sustainability and recycling of materials is as fundamentally important as their initial manufacture). Part of this operation, the New Plastics Economy Global Commitment, has recruited over 250 companies responsible for over 20% of the packaging produced on earth. The aim of the NPEGC is to refine methods of production so that plastic waste is completely reduced at its source.

ELLA DAISH

Ella Daish is a passionate campaigner bringing attention to the amount of plastic used in single-use menstrual products, and encourages women using these products to switch to more environmentally friendly options and alternatives, such as the Mooncup, which can be cleaned and reused. To provide some context, the plastic in a single sanitary towel is equivalent to four shopping bags, a fact lost on most users as the ingredients are not clearly advertised. She also draws attention to companies and governments that regulate the amount of plastic used in manufacturing sanitary products, which form a large chunk of the waste littering coastlines around the world.

MCDONALD'S

McDonald's doesn't have the best reputation when it comes to environmental business decisions, but it is important to highlight when a corporate behemoth does something right. It recently announced plans to become entirely plastic-free in their packaging and franchises by 2025. Considering the large percentage of plastic waste is caused by single-use food packaging, this is a positive step, with hopes that it becomes the new standard for its competitors to copy. As part of this global aim, McDonald's trialled a plastic-free period in one restaurant in Berlin, replacing its plastics with eco alternatives. The trial was a success, and will likely be a prototype model for McDonald's restaurants in the future.

DISNEY

The amount of single-use plastic waste contributed by theme parks is staggering, and overcoming this waste is a big step in changing the views of tourists. If the larger companies are doing it, it is hoped the smaller companies will follow. That's why the news that Disney is intending to ban the 175 million plastic straws and 13 million coffee stirrers that are generated each year at their theme parks is so important. Disneyland Paris was the first park to fulfil this pledge in April 2019, and the USA-based parks are currently preparing to do the same. Disney also pledged to reduce the amount of single-use plastics in their resorts and hotels by 80%, and to fully recycle any single-use plastics that cannot be replaced by biodegradable alternatives.

ROYAL BANK OF CANADA

The Royal Bank of Canada (RBC) is a worthy example of a business that does not actively use single-use plastic as part of its revenue generation, but is still making strong efforts to reduce its environmental footprint. The company has received a special commendation from the City of London for several measures in reducing plastic in their buildings – over 120,000 single-use items a year – as well as praise for RBC volunteers removing over 4,000 plastic bottles from the River Thames. Additionally, it has written about the financial incentives of environmentally friendly changes, and highlighted the negative impact for businesses that are slow to adopt such eco-friendly measures.

EVIAN

Bottles are the most common example of single-use plastic products that are environmentally destructive. Evian has pledged to increase the amount of recycled materials used in its production from 25% of its range to 100% by 2025. This change would relaunch Evian as an example of a circular economy that Ellen MacArthur's Foundation is aiming for with many similar brands. Evian is also attempting to encourage people to use reusable bottles with Evian water using home dispensers. These dispensers would be provided and then directly recycled by Evian, meaning comparatively little effort on the part of the consumer. Both of these measures would dramatically reduce the impact of single-use plastic bottles on the environment.

"It is hoped that the recycling mindset can be instilled in passionate fans"

JAKE AND CAROLINE DANEHY
The Fair Harbour Clothing Company

Jake and Caroline Danehy have established a popular business that turns recycled bottles into swimwear, shredding, spinning and weaving plastic into a durable material. This material is used to produce long-lasting, environmentally-friendly apparel.

TOTTENHAM HOTSPUR FOOTBALL CLUB

It is important to highlight times when established sports teams that generate passion from their fans lead the way in plastic-free experiences. Doing so encourages the culture of recycling, particularly at large events, where it is easier to feel that a global problem is being tackled with a team spirit. Tottenham Hotspur's recently opened stadium has set itself the challenge of becoming 100% single-use plastic free from day one, with recycling bins, biodegradable straws and cutlery, and bottle refilling stations. Food packaging is also becoming single-use plastic-free, and it is hoped that the recycling mindset can be instilled in passionate fans, which will then be taken back to their communities.

ICELAND

As food packaging is one of the biggest contributors to single-use plastic waste, it is vital that supermarkets provide some of the answers to countering the negative impact. In 2018 Iceland pledged to eliminate all plastic packaging from its products by 2023, which was followed by the introduction of the 'Plastic-Free Christmas Range' for 2019. Around 30 Christmas essentials will be available, giving customers the option to shop with a more sustainable mindset. It is hoped that Iceland's actions inspire other high-street chains to incorporate plastic-free alternatives in their packaging.

JACK JOHNSON - *All At Once*

Musician Jack Johnson runs the All At Once campaign, which encourages visitors to explore the ways they can reduce plastic use, support local food sustainability, and enhance their community through projects. The popular 'Top 10 plastic free tips' article has inspired thousands of people to make small positive changes, and begin thinking about their environmental footprint.

Iceland

WRITE A LETTER TO A COMPANY

Many companies are not incentivised to improve their processes unless they receive pressure from customers. If you enjoy a particular company, let them know your feelings, and they may be more inclined to review their policies

Example letter

Dear Sir/Madam,

Thank you for taking the time to read this letter. I am writing to you because your company utilises single-use plastic as part of your day-to-day operations, and I urge you to consider its use going forward. Unlike many other materials, plastic takes hundreds of years to decay, and when it does become waste, it creates chaos in the environment. Single-use plastic is one of the greatest threats to our ecology, and our society has become dependent on their use even in situations where using non-plastic materials do not present a significant inconvenience.

Even small changes made in most businesses will have a significant impact on the ecosystem at large. The easiest way to make these changes is to identify where single-use plastic most frequently appears, and then make steps to reduce its use. For example, in office cafes, take-away cups often come with single-use plastic lids. Companies can make a large reduction in the cost of both cups and recycling by simply fostering the culture of renewable drinking mugs. When a workplace culture accepts even small changes (which often happen quickly) then it becomes easier for everyone who works there to take the new attitude of sustainability home with them.

We often feel that the weight of responsible behaviour is on our shoulders as individuals, but it becomes so much easier to lift that weight when we work together. By making these changes as a company, everyone feels empowered. Additionally, when a large company (such as McDonald's or Disney) can advertise itself as tackling the plastic problem, customers will feel they are also helping when they support those businesses. Selling yourself as an environmentally-friendly business, rather than costing you money, will most likely improve your public image and drive customers to you.

There are many reasons for a successful business to adopt a healthy culture of recycling and sustainability, and I hope that you are able to do so in the near future.

Yours faithfully _____

Now use this space to write a letter a
company you feel needs to make a change.

Dear ....

....
....
....
....
....
....
....
....
....
....
....
....
....
....
....
....

Yours faithfully ....

The journey to a plastic-free world starts at home. Over the following pages, we'll explore what you can do in your own local community to make a big difference

hen a whole community, no matter how big or small, pulls together in the same direction, amazing things can happen. Villages, towns and cities across the world are uniting to help tackle the problem of plastic pollution in their own areas with big results.

Surfers Against Sewage in the UK has developed a Plastic Free Community programme; to date over 460 communities around the country have signed up to the initiative and 49 are certified as 'plastic free'. In order to get this accolade, a community must work towards achieving five key points towards reducing and eliminating plastic waste. These include having a community steering group, getting the local council on board, working with the community to ban plastic, working with local businesses to take action, and running community events, such as beach cleans.

Shining examples

This process often starts with just one passionate person. For example, in Crowthorne, Berkshire, Georgie Morris set us a group called Crowthorne Reduce Our Waste (CROW). They worked hard to get local schools to reduce the use of plastic cups, educating the whole community about recycling and waste, and introducing new recycling boxes.

Similarly, Swanage, Dorset, has achieved its plastic-free status, after a local campaign group called Sustainable Swanage was set up in May 2019. The group includes individuals, the local town council, the Chamber of Trade and Commerce, and other environmental groups. It is working hard to educate children in schools about plastic waste, as well as talking to local businesses.

In the USA, the City of Malibu, California, is committed to banning single-use plastics. It already prohibits the distribution and sale of plastic straws and cutlery items, while working with local businesses to help them adopt alternatives. There are strict local laws on the use of polystyrene foam food containers and packing materials, plastic sandbags and plastic bags. One of the elementary schools, Muse School CA, has a zero-waste sorting unit on campus and a strict policy on the use of any single-use plastics.

And there are plenty more community projects and individuals around the world that are shining examples of the difference that local projects can make towards tackling the wider plastic problem.

Getting started locally

If you're keen to get started on helping your own area become plastic free, the first port of call is seeing what resources there are already in your local community. Searching Facebook Groups is a great place to start, as most plastic-free projects will have a presence on the popular social network.

Next, see if your community has options to change your shopping habits, as this can be one of the simplest ways to reduce your plastic use. Many areas have farmer's markets, where you can pick up local fruit and veg, meat and bread, without the packaging. Just remember to take your own bags. Zero-waste shops are popping up in most major towns and cities, enabling you to fill up your own containers with things like oats, cereals, grains, seeds, nuts, flour and so on. You can often fill your own milk bottles, or refill toiletries too.

Find out about local recycling points. The kerbside recycling programme is often fairly limited, so many communities have specific recycling points for different materials. Some recycling projects can be implemented in schools or churches as a source of funding, as well as a great way to recycle. For example, crisp packets are incredibly difficult to recycle, but through a UK recycling scheme between Walkers Crisps and TerraCycle, you can drop them off at a designated recycling point. Once enough have been collected, they are all sent off for recycling into plastic pellets, which are used to build things like benches. In return, the owner of the recycling point is given points, which is converted into a financial donation to a chosen charity or school.

If there isn't anything already, then maybe you could be the one to kick-start a plastic-free revolution in your own community.

ALMOND & CO

We speak to Eleanor from zero-waste shop Almond & Co, based in Westbourne, Bournemouth, about encouraging a more sustainable, healthier lifestyle

How has the local community reacted to your zero-waste shop?

We honestly didn't expect such an amazing reception; many of our customers have been thrilled to have a shop like ours open and we attract newcomers every day. We're developing a solid number of regulars who are keen to reduce their waste, or just like to grab their favourite snack!

Since opening over six months ago, we're really starting to notice the community forming in and around the shop, bringing shopping back to how it used to be. High-street shopping, with chain shops and large supermarkets, has lost that sense of community and has become very impersonal.

Do you think that there are certain preconceptions about this kind of zero-waste shop?

Yes, there are definitely a lot of perceptions and stigma against this way of shopping. We wanted to design our shop in a way that takes it away from those assumptions and show it in a new light. We want to show that you don't have to sacrifice to reduce your waste; it can be an easier journey than you'd imagine. From the shop design, to our branding, to the products we choose, we wanted to be fresh and modern with our choices and be affordable too.

What would you say are the biggest benefits to using a shop like yours?

First and foremost I think the biggest reason is doing your bit to save the environment, protect our future generations, and sustain or bring back as much of the natural world as possible. This shop not only reduces your own waste to landfill, but it supports the smaller businesses with sustainability in mind and helps them to grow and develop into a more prominent feature in the market. Our shop encourages a healthier and more sustainable way of living with less contact with microplastics, pesticides and harmful chemicals.

Second, supporting local businesses helps the local economy, boosting the quality of life for your local area. When councils spend less removing your waste each week, more of your tax money can be spent on other more important matters.

What would be your top five tips for trying a shop like yours for the first time?

- If you have containers or bags, bring them along
- **Always ask for help if you're unsure**
- Remember to weigh your container before you fill it
- **Back and forth motion with the lever and take it easy**
- Don't sweat it! You'll be fine – worst-case scenario you spill something. Oh well!

Do you feel like you have a responsibility to inform on greater global issues, such as the Global Climate Strike?
Yes, we do feel we have a responsibility. We are always keen to promote any local sustainable practices and give them support, and talk about exciting events all over the world. But we want to emphasise the positive side rather than being negative; we want to be uplifting and supportive, rather than downing and guilt-tripping. Everybody is on their own journey and has their own capabilities. We just want to praise those who are doing their best and lead them throughout their development at their own pace.

And finally, what three simple lifestyle changes would you suggest as a starting point?
The first and biggest step would be awareness. Be aware of what you buy, where it comes from, how you buy it and what you throw away.

Second, buy items that are longer lasting and that replace single-use throwaway items. It may seem costly at first, but these changes save you money in the long run and rescue many poor-quality throwaway items from landfill.

Third, recycling is a good place to start, but a bad place to stop. Recycling can be an answer to a lot, but it certainly isn't perfect and it's quite often confusing or just not good enough. Only 9% of what we actually recycle actually gets recycled. Follow these seven Rs and focus more on what you could do before throwing it in recycling: Refuse, Reduce, Reuse, Repair, Repurpose, Recycle or Rot.

PLASTIC FREE INITIATIVES

Our handy list of resources and initiatives to help you start up a plastic-free project or make a difference in your community

PLASTIC POLLUTION COALITION

Take the 4Rs pledge to Refuse, Reduce, Reuse and Recycle, and start applying it to your own plastic usage as well as learning how to reach out to local businesses.

🌐 www.plasticpollutioncoalition.org/take-action-1

PLASTIC FREE JULY

An annual global movement to encourage people and communities to give up single-use plastics, with a whole bunch of handy resources.

🌐 www.plasticfreejuly.org

SKY OCEAN RESCUE

Lots of useful tips and resources to help you #PassOnPlastic, including weekly news roundups and handy guides to replacement products.

🌐 www.skyoceanrescue.com/passonplastic

10

TIPS FOR MAKING A DIFFERENCE LOCALLY

SET UP A FACEBOOK GROUP

If there isn't one already, set up a Facebook Group dedicated to your community. This can become a place to share ideas, as well as build a handy resource of initiatives, recycling points and schemes. Facebook is best, as a lot of people are on the network and it's easy to invite others to join.

START A RECYCLING PROGRAMME

If you know that your area lacks a recycling point for a certain type of material then you could be the one to set up a public collection point and manage it. A good place to start is the TerraCycle website (**www.**terracycle.com), available in both the UK and the USA, as well as other countries around the world.

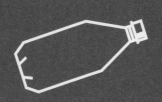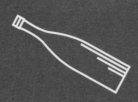

SPEAK TO LOCAL CAFES AND BARS

Pop into local cafes and bars, speak to the teams, and try to encourage them to think about the plastic they use. It's not about judging, as there are many factors to consider, but you might be able to suggest something they hadn't thought of.

JOIN A COMMUNITY GROUP

Have a look and see if there is a community group you can join. Strength in numbers can make a difference when it comes to reducing plastic waste. You'll meet like-minded people, share ideas and tackle larger-scale campaigns and projects when working as a team.

TALK TO THE PRESS

The local newspaper is a powerful ally. If you are taking part in any plastic-free project, talk to someone on the editorial team and see if they would like to cover it. Getting the word out among your community is easiest if you can use the press.

HOST A COFFEE MORNING

Gather friends and family, work colleagues, or school parents for a coffee morning with a plastic-free twist. You provide the tea and cakes, while also giving a mini workshop on plastic use and how to make small changes that have a big impact.

START A PETITION

If there is something you would like to see happen in your local community, throw yourself into creating a petition to give to your local government. They are more likely to listen with the weight of a community behind them, and it could lead to action that makes a difference.

GO TO COMMUNITY EVENTS

Many zero-waste shops and community groups will host workshops where you can learn more about living plastic free. These events are great for meeting different people with similar ethics and it could lead to new ideas that you hadn't already considered.

TALK TO YOUR SCHOOL

Educating children is important– they are our planet's future. Speak to your local school about what they can do to reduce plastic. It could be that you set up a recycling programme where they benefit from a small amount of income.

BE A ROLE MODEL

Encourage action by taking action, showing how it is possible to live a plastic-free lifestyle. If people see you taking your own water bottle, asking for coffee in your own cup, pulling out a reusable bag or refusing plastic cutlery, it will prove that anyone can make simple changes.

ORGANISE A BEACH CLEAN

Here is our quick tips guide to cleaning up your local beach

GET PERMISSION FROM
YOUR LOCAL AUTHORITY

CHOOSE A LOCATION WITH
GOOD ACCESS/PARKING

CHECK THE TIDE TIMES

PICK A DATE OFF-SEASON

PLAN WHAT WILL HAPPEN
TO THE RUBBISH COLLECTED

RECRUIT SOME VOLUNTEERS

PROMOTE THE EVENT WIDELY

HAVE A CLEAR SCHEDULE OF
WHAT WILL HAPPEN ON THE DAY

YOUR PLASTIC-FREE JOURNEY

Take some time now to reflect on how far you have come on your journey to plastic free

Write down recipes that have helped you to go plastic free, whether they are food, beauty or cleaning products record them here.

....

INGREDIENTS

....

....

....

....

....

....

....

....

....

....

....

....

....

INGREDIENTS

....

....

....

....

....

....

....

....

....

....

....

....

....

INGREDIENTS

....

....

....

....

....

....

....

....

....

....

....

....

INGREDIENTS

....

....

....

....

....

....

....

....

....

....

....

— My upcycling adventure —

Write down your own inventive upcycling methods here that have helped you to keep unavoidable plastic from the oceans.

UPCYCLING PROJECT ....

YOU WILL NEED:

....
....
....
....
....
....
....
....
....
....
....
....

DIRECTIONS:

DRAW IT HERE...

Upcycling project ....

You will need:

....

....

....

....

....

....

....

....

....

....

....

....

....

Directions:

DRAW IT HERE...

Upcycling project ....

You will need:

....
....
....
....
....
....
....
....
....
....
....
....

Directions:

DRAW IT HERE...

Upcycling project ....

You will need:

....
....
....
....
....
....
....
....
....
....
....

Directions:

. . . .
. . . .
. . . .
. . . .
. . . .
. . . .
. . . .
. . . .
. . . .
. . . .
. . . .
. . . .
. . . .

DRAW IT HERE...

What have you found to be the hardest thing about going plastic free?

What has surprised you the most about going plastic free?

....
....
....
....
....
....
....
....
....
....
....
....
....
....
....
....
....
....
....
....

5

Tips for yourself to help keep you on track with plastic-free living

1

....
....
....
....

2

....
....
....
....

3

....
....
....
....
....

4

....
....
....
....
....

5

....
....
....
....
....

Make a list of the companies and organisations that you think still have to make big plastic-free changes.

....
....
....
....
....
....
....
....
....
....
....
....
....
....
....
....
....
....
....
....
....

Have you started any plastic free
initiatives or campaigns at work or in
your community? Write about them here.

....
....
....
....
....
....
....
....
....
....
....
....
....
....
....
....
....
....
....
....
....

What are your plans for a plastic free future? How will you play a part in the plastic free movement?

....
....
....
....
....
....
....
....
....
....
....
....